NATIVE AMERICANS

Andrew Haslam

Consultant: Anne Armitage, B.A.

The American Museum in Britain

PRINCETON ■ LONDON

www.two-canpublishing.com

Published in the United States and Canada by
Two-Can Publishing LLC
234 Nassau Street, Princeton, NJ 08542

© 2001, 1995 Two-Can Publishing
Text © 1995 Alexandra Parsons
Design of models © 1995, Andrew Haslam

For information on Two-Can books and multimedia,
call 1-609-921-6700, fax 1-609-921-3349, or visit our
Web site at http://www.two-canpublishing.com

Editor: Lucy Duke
Series concept and original design: Andrew Haslam
Design: Helen McDonagh
Assistant model-maker: Sarah Davies

hc ISBN 1–58728–3085
sc ISBN 1–58728–3018

hc 1 2 3 4 5 6 7 8 9 10 02 01
sc 1 2 3 4 5 6 7 8 9 10 02 01

Photographic credits:
Eric and David Hosking: 4 (ml); Peter Newark's Western Americana: 8 (tr), 24 (tr), 45 (tl), 60 (t);
Smithsonian Institution, Museum of American History: 10 (tr), 16 (tr), 27 (tr), 30 (tr), 32 (tr), 34 (tr), 43 (tr),
46 (tl), 54 (tr); Denver Art Museum: 18 (tr); Robert Harding: 61 (br); Phoebe A. Hurst Museum of Anthropology,
The University of California at Berkeley: 26 (bl); American Museum of Natural History, courtesy
Department of Library Services: 35 (tl), 56 (bl); Range Pictures Ltd.: 4 (tr), 5 (bl), 5 (tr), 5 (br), 61 (tl);
Zefa: 39 (tr); Mel Pickering: 60 (map) (bl). All other photographs by Jon Barnes.

Printed in Hong Kong by Wing King Tong

Contents

Words marked in **bold** in the text can be found in the glossary.

Studying Native American Life _____

All human beings need food and shelter to survive. They also need things to look forward to that give their lives hope and meaning. Throughout history, different groups of people around the world have come up with their own ways of meeting these basic needs. Studying past **civilizations** can tell us how people used the resources around them to build shelters, how they farmed or found food, and how they met their spiritual needs and hopes for a better future.

△ *This man, from the Crow group in Montana, is decorating buffalo hides. Hides were used to make dwellings (see page 17).*

NATIVE AMERICANS were scattered over a vast country with a wide range of climates and **terrains**, from parched deserts in the Southwest to the frozen wastes of the North to the dense forests in the East. Those who lived in the Canadian Subarctic region had to deal with an even more extreme climate. We look at their lives, along with those of the people who lived even further north, in *Arctic Peoples*, another title in the Make it Work! History series.

TO HELP YOU study this vast area, with its wide range of different peoples, North America has been divided into seven climate regions. Each has a symbol which is used purely as a guide, when information relates to a group of people from a particular part of the country.

△ *The Shoshone of the Great Basin lived in fertile regions near the Teton Range, Wyoming.*

KEY TO THE SYMBOLS AND AREAS

 - the Plains

 - the Northeast

 - the Northwest

 - the Southwest

 - California

 - the Southeast

 - the Great Basin and Plateau

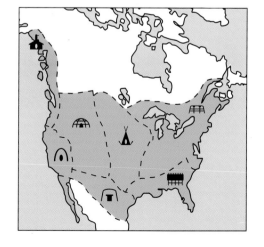

IN THIS BOOK we look at how Native Americans lived, from five hundred years ago, just before their traditional way of life was changed by the arrival of the European settlers, to the present day. We can build a picture of what this life was like from the tales told by explorers and traders. These people were among the first from other parts of the world to have any contact with Native Americans. We can also learn a great deal from the stories that have been passed down from generation to generation by the Native Americans themselves. The studies of **archaeologists** and **anthropologists** are another source of information (see page 58).

THE TRADITIONS AND LIFESTYLES of Native Americans are a vital and living part of US history. They are kept alive today by those who choose to live as their ancestors did. Many Native Americans have a strong sense of their roots, such as the Mashpees of Cape Cod.

▽ *These Plains people continue to live according to the traditions of their ancestors.*

△ *This Blackfoot chief is painting pictures showing experiences in his life (see pages 50–51).*

THE MAKE IT WORK! way of looking at history is to ask questions of the past and find answers by making replicas of the things people made. You do not have to make all the replicas in the book to understand their way of life. However, you should realize that some of the objects included are based on sacred or ceremonial traditions. Therefore, they deserve the same respect as you would give to objects that are special to your own culture or beliefs.

▽ *The Iroquois believed that these sacred masks gave the wearer the power to cure illnesses.*

Origins

There are many theories about how people arrived on the continent. Many native peoples believe they were created in North America. There are far too many versions of the story to explain here, but many of them can be found in libraries.

SOME SCIENTISTS believe that the first people came to the continent around 15,000 years ago from Siberia. They believe the people followed mammoth and giant bison over a bridge of ice or land that joined Siberia to Alaska. When the earth warmed and the ice melted, the bridge disappeared, leaving the continents separated by what is now the Bering Strait.

OTHER SCIENTISTS believe there is not enough evidence to support the Bering Strait theory. Some of these other scientists believe that the first people came to North America from Africa by boat. Whatever the real story may be, it is true that in 1500, when the first Europeans arrived on the continent, there were at least 600 nations living in North America. Today, there are more than 500, including Alaskan natives such as the Aleuts and the Inuit.

▷ *This map shows the location of some of the main **nations**. Many of these peoples are discussed in this book.*

PACIFIC NORTHWEST
(warm, wet summers; cool, wet winters)

Haida
Tlingit
Chinook
Nootka
Kwakiutl

CALIFORNIA
(hot and dry all year round)

Chumash
Miwok
Maidu
Karok
Pomo
Yahi

SOUTHWEST
(hot and dry all year round)

Pueblos
Apache
Navajo
Yuma
Hopi
Zuni

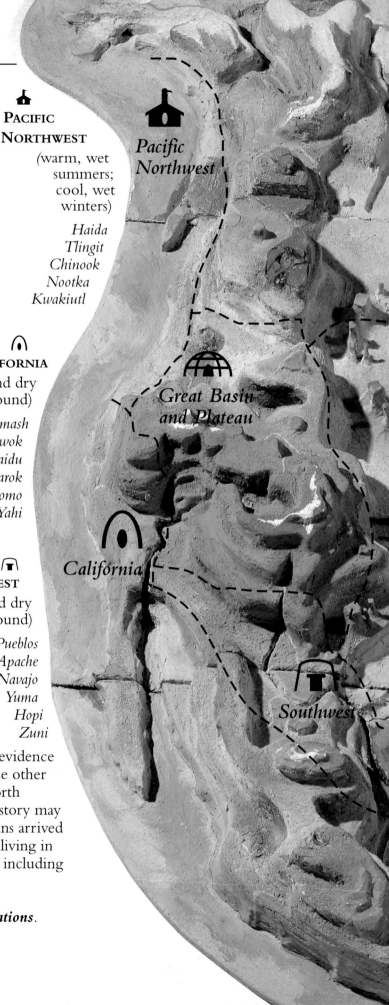

Pacific Northwest

Great Basin and Plateau

California

Southwest

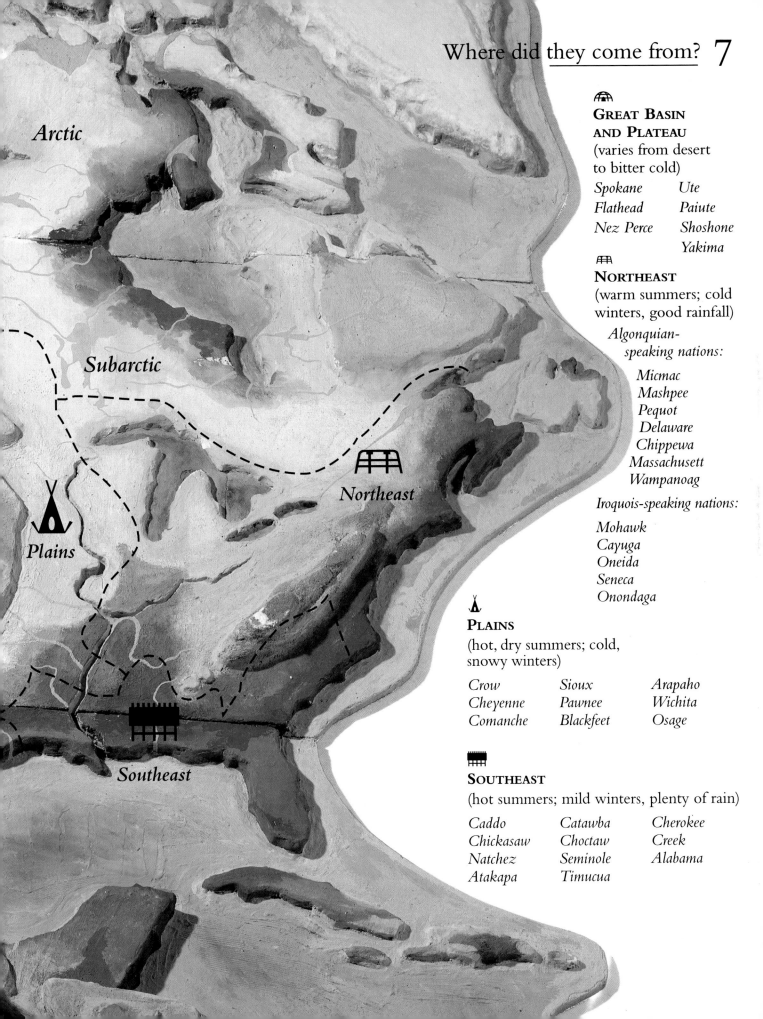

**GREAT BASIN
AND PLATEAU**
(varies from desert
to bitter cold)

Spokane   Ute
Flathead   Paiute
Nez Perce   Shoshone
               Yakima

NORTHEAST
(warm summers; cold
winters, good rainfall)

*Algonquian-
speaking nations:*

Micmac
Mashpee
Pequot
Delaware
Chippewa
Massachusett
Wampanoag

Iroquois-speaking nations:

Mohawk
Cayuga
Oneida
Seneca
Onondaga

PLAINS
(hot, dry summers; cold,
snowy winters)

Crow   Sioux   Arapaho
Cheyenne   Pawnee   Wichita
Comanche   Blackfeet   Osage

SOUTHEAST
(hot summers; mild winters, plenty of rain)

Caddo   Catawba   Cherokee
Chickasaw   Choctaw   Creek
Natchez   Seminole   Alabama
Atakapa   Timucua

Arctic

Subarctic

Plains

Northeast

Southeast

Clothing

Although many people think of traditional Native American dress as fringed tunics, feather headdresses, and braided hair, this is not what everyone wore. Tunics were worn by some Plains groups. As with everything in Native American life, the clothes people wore depended on where and how they lived. Those in northern and eastern areas needed warm clothing. Many western and southern Native Americans wore little clothing, decorating their bodies instead with tattoos. Hunters made clothing from animal hides and fur, while gatherers and farmers used plant fibers.

△ *Wolf Robe, of the Southern Cheyenne, is wearing feathers from the golden eagle. This photograph was taken in 1909.*

WARBONNETS were made from the tail feathers of the golden eagle. Warriors proved their bravery by collecting feathers from the fierce, powerful birds. They cut and colored them in different ways to let others know about their fighting skills (see page 46).

wearer wounded

wearer wounded many times

*wearer **counted coup** four times*

wearer cut enemy's throat

wearer killed enemy

MAKE A SIOUX HEADDRESS

You will need: canvas or plain fabric, 12-15 feathers, tape, glue, colored ribbons, paint, paintbrush, scissors, hook-and-loop fasteners

1 Paint the tips of the feathers and wrap tape around the quills.

2 Cut a canvas strip long enough to fit around your head with some overlap and twice as wide as the headband will be. Turn in and glue the edges, then fold the strip in half lengthwise. Mark and paint a design on it, as shown.

3 Glue inside the folded strip, leaving small, evenly spaced pockets for the feathers. Glue a feather into each pocket. Decorate the headdress with colored streamers made from the ribbons.

BODY PAINT made from reddish brown mud, called ocher, mixed with animal fat was used by woodland groups to paint their bodies. The designs and colors showed that people belonged to a special group, or told of their deeds or dreams. Body paint had a practical use, too. The grease in the paint protected their skin from the sun, wind, cold, and stinging and biting insects.

TATTOOS were worn by people in the hot, sunny Southeast and in California. They wore few clothes, but used tattoos to decorate and express themselves. They used needles made from cactus spines or slivers of bone to prick patterns on their skin.

HAIRSTYLES were important ways to look different but still fit in with national traditions. Some groups smeared their hair with mud and sculpted it into elaborate shapes. Many warriors shaved their heads so they looked fierce and threatening. They sometimes tied a stiff tuft of animal hair, known as a **roach**, in the center.

TWEEZERS made from shells, wood, or bone were used by men to pluck the hair from their faces. They rarely grew beards or moustaches.

HATS were made by many Native Americans, using assorted materials. Californians wove sun hats from reeds and decorated them with poppy flowers. In the Northwest Pacific, hats were woven from cedar bark. Woodland peoples wore headbands made from fur or hide, or turbanlike sashes woven from plant fibers.

4 Glue strips of the fasteners to the ends of the headband so you can secure it around your head.

THE MEN OF THE GREAT PLAINS wore only a piece of soft **buckskin** passed between their legs and tied with a belt. In winter, when the weather was fiercely cold, they added fitted, thigh-length leggings and a knee-length tunic.

WOMEN'S LEGGINGS were held up with garters just below the knee. Dresses were often made of two deer skins sewn together, with the animals' legs making natural sleeves. In the chillier North, both men and women wore robes made of softened buffalo skin with the hair left on.

CHILDREN wore nothing in the summer and child-sized versions of adult clothes in winter. Tunics, leggings, and dresses were often decorated with quillwork or beaded embroidery.

△ *Ute warriors like this man (right) wore magnificent breastplates of bone, porcupine quills, and shells and decorated themselves with body paint.*

MAKE A PLAINS OUTFIT

You will need: burlap or similar fabric, long ruler, felt-tip pens, scissors, glue gun or stapler, paints, chamois leather or duster, beads

1 To make the leggings, fold fabric in half to make a double thickness. Measure and mark the trouser shape, as shown, using a long ruler or a straight piece of wood.

2 Cut through the two thicknesses of fabric. Glue or staple the seams (or sew them), adding strips of frayed fabric to the outer seams to look like fringes.

3 Paint designs directly onto the fabric, then glue or sew on a triangular piece of chamois leather or scrap of leftover fabric. This represents the buckskin loincloth.

△ *Clothes with a lot of beadwork were very heavy and were usually worn just for special occasions.*

ANIMAL SKINS used for clothes had to be softened. This skilled work was done by women, who rubbed the skin with a mixture of animal brains, liver, ashes, and fat. They soaked it in water and pulled, stretched, or even chewed the leather until it became soft buckskin. Clothes made from skins were dry-cleaned by rubbing them in clay and chalk to absorb the dirt.

⚠ MAKE A PAIR OF MOCCASINS

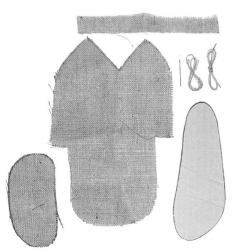

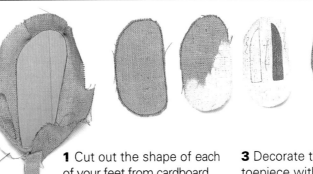

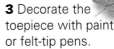

You will need: burlap or similar fabric, cardboard, felt-tip pens, paints, thin string, a darning needle, scissors

1 Cut out the shape of each of your feet from cardboard. Use the cardboard soles as a guide to cut larger, irregular-shaped pieces as shown, then cut a toepiece and a thin strip.

2 Fold, and use string to sew the fabric around the cardboard soles, folding in the wings. Use the strip to join the two pieces at the heel.

3 Decorate the toepiece with paint or felt-tip pens.

4 Sew the toepiece into position with string, as shown. Finish off your moccasins by stitching around the top edge, starting and finishing at the heel end. Then you can adjust the fit by tightening the string.

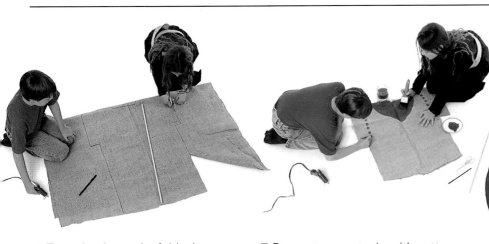

4 To make the tunic, fold a long piece of fabric to make a double thickness, with the fold at the top. Measure and mark the shape, as shown, then cut it out through both thicknesses of fabric. Cut a neck hole at the top. Glue, staple, or sew the seams, as before.

5 Decorate your tunic with patterns, using paints or felt-tip pens. Add fringes, beads, or feathers. You will find suggestions for designs and colors on pages 36-37.

6 To make a woman's outfit, make a long tunic (see photo on page 13).

⚠ **MOCCASINS** were made in various styles for different uses. Some were low cut and others came almost to the knee. Work shoes had hard **rawhide** soles, while shoes worn at home were soft-soled. Moccasins helped protect people's feet from sharp stones, spiky plants, poisonous snakes, and stinging insects.

▷ *Plains warriors carried spears and hide shields (see page 47) and wore elaborate headdresses for ceremonial occasions.*

JEWELRY AND ORNAMENTS were made from many different materials. Coastal peoples used shells, while those on the Plains used quills from birds' feathers and from porcupine spines colored with vegetable and mineral dyes. Northern groups had long been making copper necklaces. Once southern groups had learned how to work silver, they made beautiful ornaments with traditional designs.

GLASS AND CERAMIC BEADS brought by Europeans were very popular because cutting, drilling, and polishing stones and shells to make beads was hard work. The most important beads were **wampum**, made in the Northeast from ground, polished shells. They were used for decoration, keeping records, sending messages, making medicine, and as money.

buffalo-horn helmet

ceremonial headdress

shell decoration

decorated goat-hair blanket

deerskin apron

woolen tunic

🐚 Nez Perce   🐚 Chumash   🏠 Tlingit   🛖 Navajo

🐚 **THE NEZ PERCE** lived in high plateau country to the west of the Rocky Mountains. The weather was cold and no crops grew. People relied on gathering roots, berries, and nuts and on fishing and hunting. Nez Perce warriors wore ermine-tail and buffalo-horn helmets, and buckskin war shirts with porcupine-quill decoration and horsehair tassels.

🏠 **THE TLINGIT**, like other Native Americans in the Northwest, led comfortable lives (see page 24). The winter months were a time of festivals and fun. Party outfits included blankets woven from goat hair and plant-fiber tunics. It rained often, so people wore waterproof hats, tightly woven from spruce roots. Their tunics were good rainwear, too, drying out more quickly than a soggy deerskin ever could.

THE CHUMASH lived near the California coast, in an area with plenty of food and a warm climate all year round. Women wore two deerskin apron-type garments around their waists. The back skirts were painted and decorated with shells, and the front aprons were fringed. Shoes were made of plant fiber. Women decorated their faces to show the family from which they came.

MOHAWK WARRIORS wore fringed animal-hide cloths around their waists, with leggings and moccasins. They had tattoos on their foreheads that declared their bravery in battle, and sometimes wore fan-shaped roaches made of animal hair. Their war clubs were carved from a wood so hard that it was known as ironwood.

feather decoration

bead necklace

hide cloth

leggings

fringed tunic

Sioux

Mohawk

Seminole

THE NAVAJO herded sheep, introduced by Spanish settlers, and therefore had access to wool. They wove blankets, often boldly striped and decorated with patterns unique to them. Women wore simple tunic dresses made from two pieces of blanket tied at the waist with a woven sash. Leggings, soft moccasins, and beads and buckles of silver completed their traditional outfits.

THE SEMINOLE was a group formed by the Creek people and others from different areas. They gradually came together in the Southeast after Europeans began to settle in North America. Their clothes were influenced by early European styles of dress, which they decorated with their own elaborate patchwork and beadwork.

Housing

The climate of the vast North American landmass varies between year-round snow and ice in the frozen North and scorching heat in the deserts of the Southwest. As the Native Americans settled into their homelands, they built houses that were suited to the climate and natural features of their particular region. They used any available materials.

A LEAN-TO was a temporary shelter built by Subarctic peoples from sticks, leaves, or bark.

🏠 **A PLANK HOUSE** was a winter home for the peoples of the Northwest. It was made from hand-split planks fixed onto a frame made from logs, and it was usually rectangular.

▲ **TEPEES** were perfect homes for the mobile, buffalo-hunting Plains peoples. They were portable and were made of buffalo skins and wooden poles.

WICKIUPS were cone-shaped or domed houses built around frames made from wooden poles, often covered with grass or rush. They were the homes of many Great Basin people.

CLIFF DWELLINGS, or **pueblos,** were the homes of native groups in the Southwest, where humans have lived for at least 6,000 years and a settled farming culture thrived. Houses made of mud, rubble, and blocks of stone were called pueblos (meaning "villages") by the Spanish, who arrived in the sixteenth century.

REED HOUSES were made from reed mats covering a wooden pole frame. Inside, there was often a central pit for a fire and a smoke hole in the roof. These conical houses were often found in the Southwest and in California.

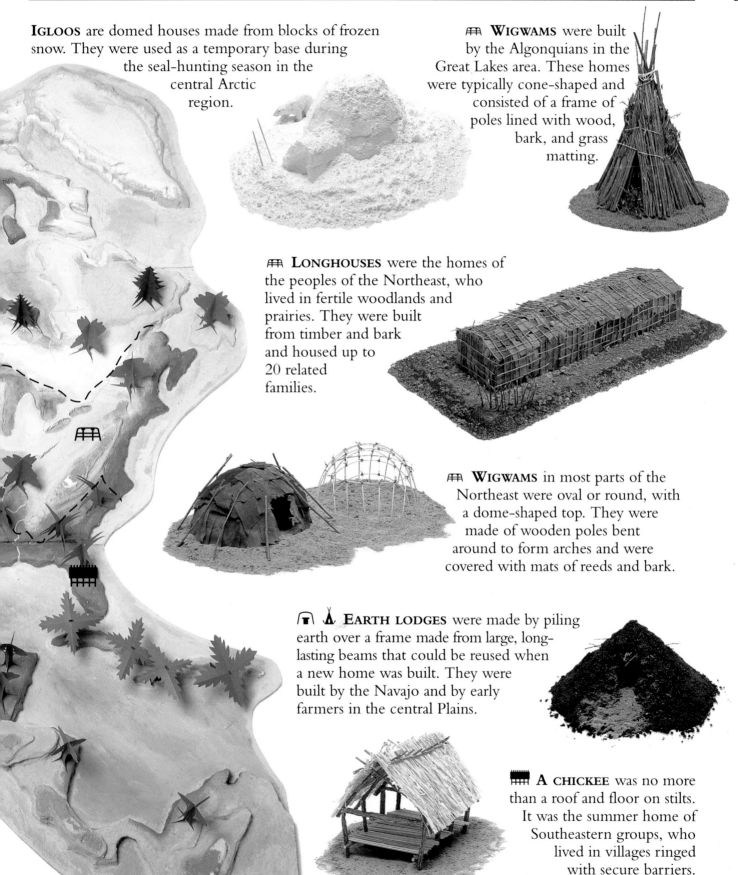

IGLOOS are domed houses made from blocks of frozen snow. They were used as a temporary base during the seal-hunting season in the central Arctic region.

WIGWAMS were built by the Algonquians in the Great Lakes area. These homes were typically cone-shaped and consisted of a frame of poles lined with wood, bark, and grass matting.

LONGHOUSES were the homes of the peoples of the Northeast, who lived in fertile woodlands and prairies. They were built from timber and bark and housed up to 20 related families.

WIGWAMS in most parts of the Northeast were oval or round, with a dome-shaped top. They were made of wooden poles bent around to form arches and were covered with mats of reeds and bark.

EARTH LODGES were made by piling earth over a frame made from large, long-lasting beams that could be reused when a new home was built. They were built by the Navajo and by early farmers in the central Plains.

A CHICKEE was no more than a roof and floor on stilts. It was the summer home of Southeastern groups, who lived in villages ringed with secure barriers.

ᛉ **SOME PEOPLES**, such as the Cheyenne and the Sioux, spent much of their lives on the move across the central Plains following the buffalo, which were their main source of food. Their tepees were pleasant, practical homes that were cool in summer, warm in winter, strong enough to stand up to fierce winds, and big enough for the family and all its belongings.

ᛉ **TEPEES** were sometimes made from fourteen buffalo hides sewn together with buffalo sinews (the tough, stringy fibers that attach muscle to bone). Needles were carved from buffalo bone.

△ *These Comanche women, photographed in 1890, have pegged out buffalo skins so they can scrape them clean.*

ᛉ **MAKE A TEPEE**

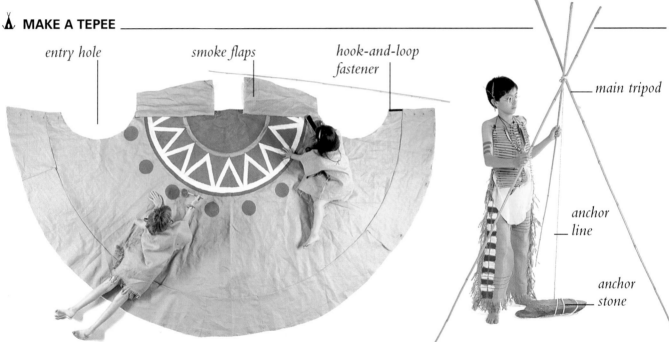

entry hole   smoke flaps   hook-and-loop fastener

main tripod

anchor line

anchor stone

You will need: old blankets or double sheets, thumbtack, string, scissors, garden stakes (8 feet long), stapler or needle and thread, white glue, rope or clothesline, paints, paintbrushes, hook-and-loop fasteners, short sticks, stones

1 Cut a piece of string 20 inches shorter than your stakes and use it like a compass to draw a semicircle on the fabric. Tack one end to the center of the long side of the fabric and tie a pencil to the other end. Swing the string around and mark an arc.

2 Cut small, matching semicircular openings for the entry hole, as shown. Sew or staple strips of hook-and-loop fasteners on either side of the hole for fastening the tepee over the stakes.

3 Cut out the smoke flaps as shown and staple or sew them in place. Make a small triangular pocket in the top inside corner of each flap (see step 7).

4 Paint the cover, adding about one part glue to one part paint to make it waterproof. Use the scissors to make holes for the tent pegs around the base.

5 Make the tepee frame using 3 stakes. Tie them together with the thicker ends at the top. Use a heavy object as a weight to secure the other end of the rope, as shown.

6 Wrap the cover carefully around the stake tripod and secure it by sticking the strips of fasteners together. People such as the Cheyenne and Crow used tepee pins to hold the covers of their tepees in place. You can make your own pins using short sticks. Make holes in both layers of the tepee cover, where it overlaps, and thread the pins through the holes as shown.

THE MAIN TRIPOD was tied together on the ground, then lifted upright using an anchor line made from rawhide. A family tepee was usually 16 feet high and just under 16 feet in diameter, which is about as big as a medium-sized room.

SPECIAL PATTERNS AND COLORS were used by each group to paint their tepees. People would adapt the national pattern for their own family or region. The number of dots, for instance, may represent the number of lakes in the area. The women did all the painting, using ground-up rock and colored soil mixed with buffalo blood.

7 Slide more poles inside the tepee cover to make the frame stronger. Secure the base, using short sticks as tent pegs. Push one end of a stake into each smoke flap pocket to prop the flaps open. Finally, cut out and pin on a door flap to fit over the entry hole.

ON RAINY DAYS a tepee's smoke flaps were closed and fastened with tepee pins.

MEN AND WOMEN had their own particular responsibilities. Women made and put up tepees, while men kept lookout. Two women would take about an hour to erect one tepee.

BLACK ELK, of the Sioux nation, said: 'Our tepees were round like the nests of birds and these were always set in a circle, the nation's hoop, a nest of many nests where the Great Spirit meant for us to hatch our children.'

smoke flaps

entry hole

tepee cover   *tepee pin*

INSIDE THE TEPEE people slept on piles of warm, furry buffalo skins. When they gathered around the fire, they had comfortable wooden backrests to lean against. Native Americans stored their food, medicine, and clothes in soft hide bags, embroidered with elaborate patterns. A typical Plains family had many horses, but few possessions other than the things they really needed.

EXTRA INSULATION against wind and cold was often provided by a decorative inner lining that trapped a pocket of warm air between it and the outside layer to keep the inside temperature comfortable.

THE FIREPLACE, sometimes raised on a slab of stone, was the main source of light and heat. The supply of firewood was never allowed to run low.

WARNING: DO NOT LIGHT FIRES IN A MODEL TEPEE

△ *This soft buffalo-hide tepee liner belonged to a Cheyenne family. Tepee liners were not hung all around the tent, but were attached at the points where the wind whistled through, positioned at waist height to protect people from drafts as they sat around the fire or lay in bed.*

VENTILATION was provided during warm summer weather by rolling up the sides of the tepee to let air in.

BACKRESTS were used only by the men of the family. The firm but springy supports were made of wooden slats lashed together with leather strips.

EVERYTHING HAD ITS OWN PLACE inside the tepee. The beds were placed on either side of the fire. The fire itself was set in front of the central anchor rope. Backrests were positioned against the sides, and a supply of firewood was kept just inside the door.

△ **A STRICT CODE** of manners meant that a person could not just walk into a friend's tepee. There were rules to follow:

● If the door flap was open, visitors could enter, but if it was closed, they had to wait to be invited in.

● The male visitor went in first, moved around to the right, and waited for the host to offer him a seat on his left. Women could then enter, and they turned left.

● Men were allowed to sit cross-legged, but women were not.

● Guests invited to a meal had to bring their own spoons and bowls and eat everything their host provided for them.

● No one was allowed to walk between the fire and another person.

● When the host lit his pipe, it was the signal for the guests to go home.

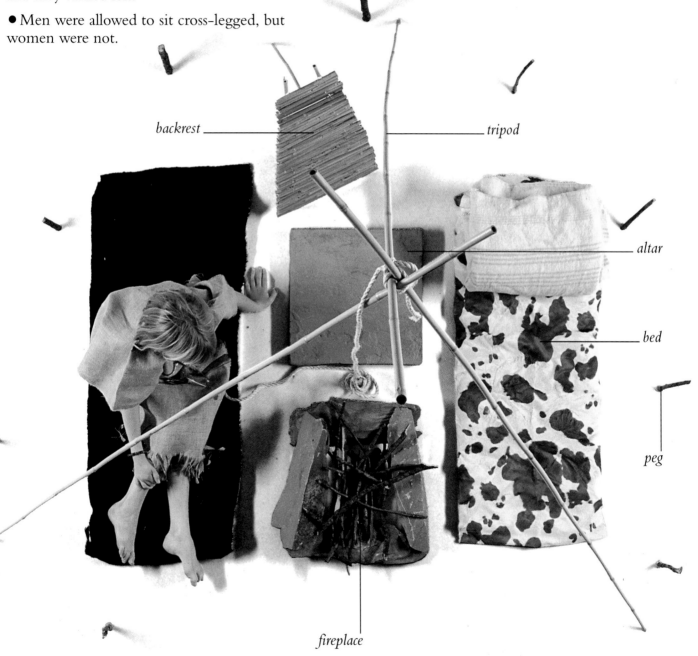

backrest

tripod

altar

bed

peg

fireplace

THE IROQUOIS settled on the East Coast, in what is now southern Ontario, Quebec, and New York State. They built villages and farmed the rich land, where there was plenty of firewood and clear, clean water from the many rivers and springs. They lived in close-knit groups, and their villages were collections of enormous longhouses surrounded by high, protective fences, or palisades, made of sharp stakes. But these villages were not really permanent. Early farming methods exhausted the land after about 20 years. When the crops would no longer grow, the people moved on and rebuilt in a more fertile place.

LONGHOUSES were as high as they were wide. The average size was 65 feet long, 20 feet high by 20 feet wide. One house was home to a group of related fireside families. Each family had its own space along the side of the house and shared a fire in the central corridor with the family opposite. There was a door at each end, but no windows. Smoke from the fires eventually found its way out through a series of ventilation holes in the roof, but the inside was very smoky. As a result, many longhouse people suffered from eye trouble and became blind as they grew old.

MAKE A LONGHOUSE

fire corridor   *sleeping platform*

You will need: 3 lengths of wood (2 thick, 1 thin), thick and thin twigs, plywood base (26 x 16 in.), wood filler, soil, glue, scraps of fabric or leather

1 Make sleeping platforms and a fire corridor by laying the strips of wood parallel to one another, with the thinner one in the middle.

2 Cut some thick twigs to the same length and, spacing them equally, glue them upright on the board.

3 Mix the filler with water to make a paste and spread it over the board and platforms. Sprinkle the soil over the wet filler so that it sticks.

4 Cut beams from thick twigs to make the roof frame. Stick pairs of beams together to make the roof shape, as shown, and glue them in place on top of each pair of upright posts. Make a framework of thin twigs over the walls and roof to form a support for the bark tiles.

5 Cut the fabric or leather roughly into squares. Glue them to the framework in overlapping layers, starting at the bottom so that there are no cracks for rain to seep in. Glue a lattice of thin twigs over the tiles.

6 Make a palisade from sharpened twigs. Stick them to the base board, sharp ends up and pointing outward, to form a defensive wall around the longhouse.

⌂ MAKE AN EARTH LODGE

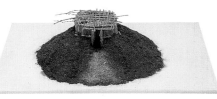

You will need: base board (16 x 16 in.), thick and thin twigs, moss or leaves, soil, glue

1 Cut all the thick twigs to the same length and glue upright to the base board in a square. Leave a small gap in one side for the doorway.

2 Lay a lattice of thinner twigs over the top and cover it with moss or leaves. Pile soil over the frame to form a cone, leaving a clear pathway to the door.

When Navajo people built their earth lodges, they hammered the frame posts into the ground next to each other to form a solid wall of timber. They made the doorway shoulder-width, so the home was easier to defend. The houses of the northeastern Wampanoags varied in shape and were covered with bark or mats .

bark tiles

upright beam

roof beam

framework of thin poles to hold tiles down in high winds

palisade to defend the longhouse village

⌗ **LONGHOUSE BUILDING MATERIALS** were mainly wood and bark. The outer frame was made from thick posts, firmly driven into the ground. Horizontal beams were lashed in place with strong bark fibers. The roof frame was made from thinner poles and the whole house was covered with overlapping tiles of ash or elm tree bark.

⌗ **THE PALISADE** was made from stakes that were spaced so that the distance between them was just the width of a person's shoulders. Villagers could come and go freely, but attacking warriors had to thread their way through with their arms pinned to their sides, making it very difficult for them to use their weapons.

Family Life

A village in the Plains was made up of groups of families, or **clans**, who often traced their relationship to one another through the women of the family. There could be 50 or more loosely related clans in one group, which occupied an area of land, or territory. The most important ties were not to the group but to the family: the mother, father, and children who shared a home and a fireside.

△ **TEPEES** were set up with their entrances facing east to keep out the winds that usually blew across the open Plains from the west. They were grouped according to family relationships.

▽ *Tepee villages were built on carefully chosen sites, close to a river or stream and sheltered from the wind wherever possible.*

tepee frame

strips of buffalo meat curing in the sun

door flap

buffalo chips for making a fire

△ **LIFE ON THE MOVE** meant a tough routine for those who hunted buffalo in the vast, dry, windy central Plains. They spent their lives packing up camp, dragging or carrying their possessions, and setting up camp all over again. But their efforts were repaid by a constant supply of food, clothing, and shelter from the buffalo.

△ **VILLAGES** were run by chiefs and elders, who were chosen by fellow villagers to offer advice, rather than to tell people what to do. Most people could do as they chose, as long as they worked for the general good, for villages shared their **livelihood**. Men hunted and fought, while women cleaned skins, made clothes, put up tepees, and cooked.

colored streamers for sending messages to the spirit world

smoke flap

wooden tepee pins holding the tepee cover in place

cooking pot made from a buffalo stomach

prepared buffalo skins pegged out to dry

▲ **MARRIAGE** for some Plains peoples was a kind of sharing partnership for the livelihood of the village. Because hunting and war claimed the lives of so many men, there were usually more women than men in a clan. Thus it was not uncommon for a man to have more than one wife. They would split the chores of their household, which made the lives of the women easier.

*tepee cover with painted **symbols** telling of the spirits or of battles fought by the owner*

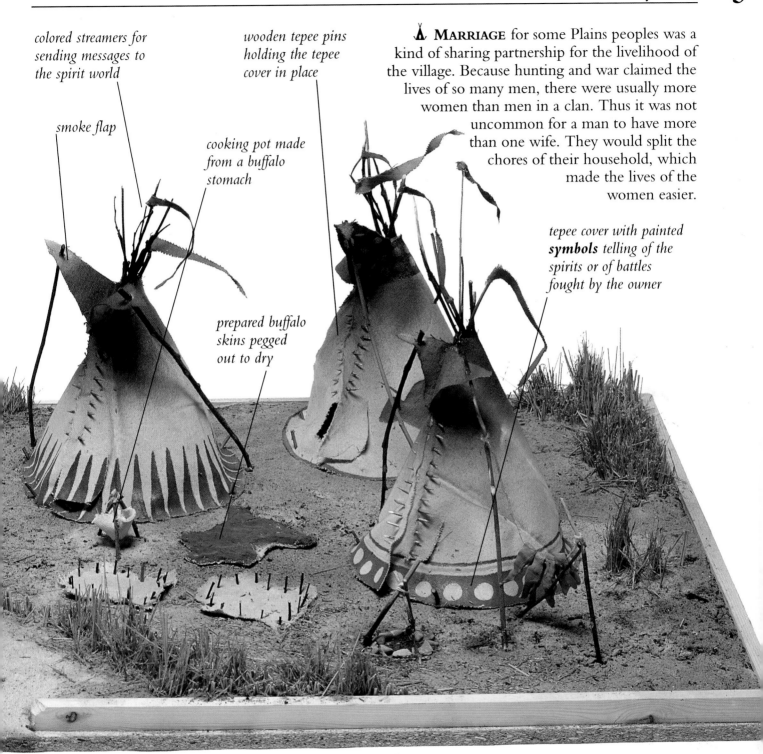

▲ **CHILDREN** were educated through playing with toy bows, tepees, and dolls and learning from their elders about the life they would lead as adults. They were always expected to behave in a way that would bring no danger or dishonor to their clan or group. They learned very quickly not to cry or make a fuss if an enemy was near.

▲ **WARRIORS** were usually men, but some women also fought enemies and hunted buffalo. Men thought so highly of one Crow warrior, Woman Chief, that they were too scared to ask to marry her. She "married" four women so she would have someone to look after her tepee. If a man preferred to work at home, no one minded.

THE PEOPLES in the Pacific Northwest lived in fishing villages along the coast. There were nearly 50 groups there, leading well-ordered, comfortable lives. They were the richest peoples in the land, thanks to a flourishing trade in dried and smoked fish and finely woven basketware. These were the Native Americans most concerned with showing their social rank and wealth.

WOODEN HOUSES were strung out in villages along the coastline, with all the houses facing the sea. Each plank house was home to several related families, and the carved **totem poles** outside let everyone know the histories of the families living there.

△ *Totem poles were made by skilled carvers of the Northwestern groups. Their main function was to record family crests and glorious moments of family history.*

♙ MAKE A PLANK HOUSE AND TOTEM POLE

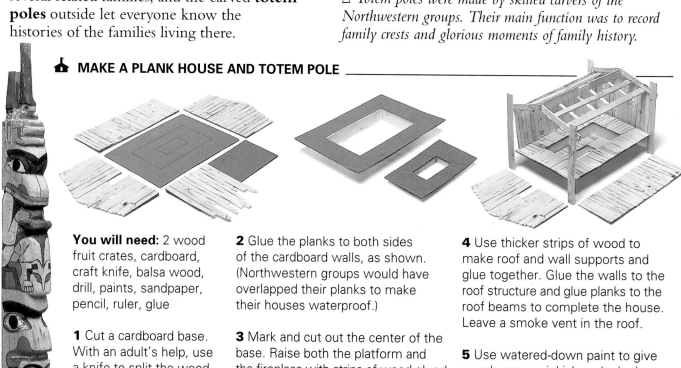

◁ *Animals on totem poles represented the various characteristics of family members.*

You will need: 2 wood fruit crates, cardboard, craft knife, balsa wood, drill, paints, sandpaper, pencil, ruler, glue

1 Cut a cardboard base. With an adult's help, use a knife to split the wood from the crates along the grain to make planks.

2 Glue the planks to both sides of the cardboard walls, as shown. (Northwestern groups would have overlapped their planks to make their houses waterproof.)

3 Mark and cut out the center of the base. Raise both the platform and the fireplace with strips of wood glued at right angles to the edges. Cover all exposed cardboard with planks.

4 Use thicker strips of wood to make roof and wall supports and glue together. Glue the walls to the roof structure and glue planks to the roof beams to complete the house. Leave a smoke vent in the roof.

5 Use watered-down paint to give your house a pinkish cedar look. Paint the smoke vent black.

6 To make a totem pole, cut a piece of balsa wood a little taller than your house. Sand it to make a flattened cylinder shape and drill a hole for the doorway as shown.

7 Draw your design and carve the lines with a craft knife. Glue on extra pieces for wings or beaks. Sand and paint your totem pole and glue it to the front of your plank house.

🏠 **CEDAR WOOD** was easy to carve and hollow out to make canoes. The stringy bark gave fiber for making baskets, ropes, and clothes. Northwestern groups reasoned that these trees must be on Earth to help humans.

🏠 **RAINFALL** is high in the Pacific Northwest, and the winters are cold. Plank houses were made of overlapping cedar planks so that the rain ran off. They had no windows, just a hole in the roof that could be closed with a wooden shutter.

🏠 **A PLANK HOUSE** was home for up to six families, related through the women. Their shared living space was about 160 square feet, with a sunken area in the center where children played and women cooked. A sleeping platform around the edge was divided into family spaces, with the most important family at the back and the lowliest near the drafty door.

🏠 **A POTLATCH** was organized by a Northwestern family to celebrate a special event, such as a wedding. They put on a lavish feast and gave their guests many valuable gifts, including canoes, slaves, furs, and blankets. The more gifts a host gave, the higher his or her status rose. The guests who received the most then had to throw an even greater potlatch. Among the Northwestern peoples, being wealthy meant being more important. People used potlatches to show how rich they were, and to settle old rivalries. Through potlatching, they could force their rivals to give away everything they owned.

smoke hole in roof

totem pole

Food

Native Americans lived on a healthy diet of meat or fish, grain, nuts, fruit, and other food plants. Most of them had learned how to preserve meat and fish by drying or smoking, so there were always emergency supplies if the hunters came back empty-handed.

△ BUFFALO HUNTING was exhausting and lonely. It took up most of the day, but it was necessary for survival. Tracking and killing large animals on foot was dangerous. To succeed, men had to be in tune with nature and understand the animals they hunted. They sometimes dressed in buffalo skins and moved among the herd. Hunters only took what they needed and never killed animals just for the sake of it.

△ *Ishi, of the California Yahi, photographed in 1914 making a salmon harpoon, or leister.*

🏛 ANIMALS that provided food were treated with great respect. A ceremony was held for the first salmon caught in each run. It was taken to a special altar, welcomed with speeches, and cooked with great care. Some Native Americans believed that there were people living in the sea who took the form of salmon each year. If they were not treated properly, they might never come again.

fence to keep salmon from swimming farther upstream

🏛 FISHERMEN on the Northeast Coast used harpoons, nets, and traps to catch millions of salmon that returned every summer from the ocean to lay eggs in the rivers where they were born. There was also an ocean full of fish, seals, and whales, and plenty of shellfish and birds' eggs along the shore.

🏛 MAKE A SALMON TRAP

You will need: dried grasses, paint, plywood base (10 x 18 in.), stones, twigs, sand, craft knife, glue

1 Paint a river on the board. Make sand banks on both sides, dotted with dried grasses and pebbles.

2 Build a fence across the river. Glue the crosspieces to the supports.

(Native Americans who fished would have pushed the supports into the ground and tied the sticks with sinews.)

The fence stops the salmon from swimming farther upstream. They will never turn back, so they struggle and leap against the fence, while more fish swim up behind them.

3 Make trapping gates in the same way as the fence. Bend twigs to make the rounded ends of the tunnel-shaped pens. Add to the fence.

Men with spears would have waded into the killing pen. Any fish not harpooned at once were swept back by the current into the trapping gates and collected in the pens.

▦ **PREPARING AND PRESERVING FISH** was done by the women. The rich fish oil was highly prized and used as grease for cooking and for lamps. It was traded along "grease trails" down the coast and over the mountains.

▷ *Fish traps were made to much the same design all over the Northeast and Subarctic.*

killing pen

trapping
gate

tunnel-
shaped pen

▦ **SOUTHEASTERN HUNTERS** caught small animals in traps. They used blowpipes and poison darts to hunt deer. Some could knock birds from the sky with **bolas** made from stones tied to a line of sinew, which they whirled around their heads and then let fly.

THE THREE MAIN FOOD CROPS grown by Native Americans were corn, beans, and squash. Farmers used tools made of wood or bone. Men turned the earth and women planted the seeds.

RUBBING STICKS TOGETHER to make a fire took so long that fires were often left smoldering all day. Many hunters traveled with a slow-burning rope so they had a quick way of lighting a fire when they set up camp.

🏠 RICH SOIL meant good crops, and farmers believed in putting something back into the earth in thanks for what came out. The Iroquois, for example, put herring into the ground before they sowed corn. The nutrients in the fish made the soil much richer.

🏠 A TYPICAL IROQUOIS MEAL included roasted meat, raw salad, baked pumpkin, and corn dumplings. Families ate just once a day, before noon. Meals were eaten in silence, standing or squatting on the ground. Men ate first, and women and children ate what was left. Children were told that if they did not thank their parents for each meal, they would be punished with a stomachache.

🍴 MAKE HOPI BOILED CORN CAKES

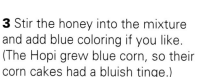

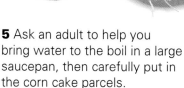

You will need: 30 corn husks (the outer part of a corncob), 1 cup of cornmeal, half a cup of honey, blue food coloring (optional)

1 With an adult's help, boil the corn husks until they are soft. Drain them and let them cool.

2 Put cornmeal in a bowl and, while stirring, gradually add a cup of boiling water, until mixture is like thick custard.

3 Stir the honey into the mixture and add blue coloring if you like. (The Hopi grew blue corn, so their corn cakes had a bluish tinge.)

4 Open out the corn husks and drop 2 spoonfuls of corn mixture into the center of about 20 of them. Fold them neatly into parcels. Shred the remaining husks and use the shreds to tie up the parcels.

5 Ask an adult to help you bring water to the boil in a large saucepan, then carefully put in the corn cake parcels.

6 Boil the parcels for 15 to 20 minutes, then take them out with a slotted spoon. Let them cool before you unwrap and eat them.

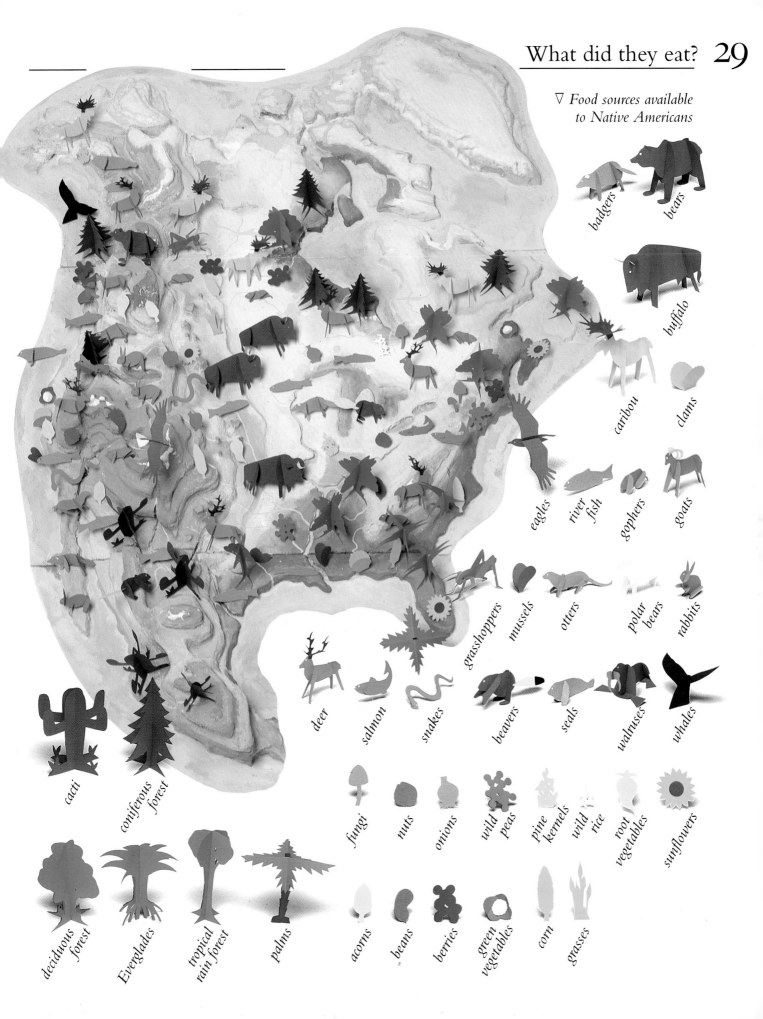

▽ Food sources available to Native Americans

badgers

bears

buffalo

caribou

clams

eagles

river fish

gophers

goats

grasshoppers

mussels

otters

polar bears

rabbits

deer

salmon

snakes

beavers

seals

walruses

whales

cacti

coniferous forest

fungi

nuts

onions

wild peas

pine kernels

wild rice

root vegetables

sunflowers

deciduous forest

Everglades

tropical rain forest

palms

acorns

beans

berries

green vegetables

corn

grasses

Sports and Leisure

Most Native American games were a preparation for life, and many were ceremonial. Men played vigorous team games to help prepare themselves for war and hunting games to sharpen their skills. Women played games of skill and chance, using their everyday work tools. Both men and women also liked to sing as they placed bets in games of chance. They made music to summon up good spirits and good luck.

△ *Lacrosse* players were allowed two sticks each.

MAKE A LACROSSE STICK

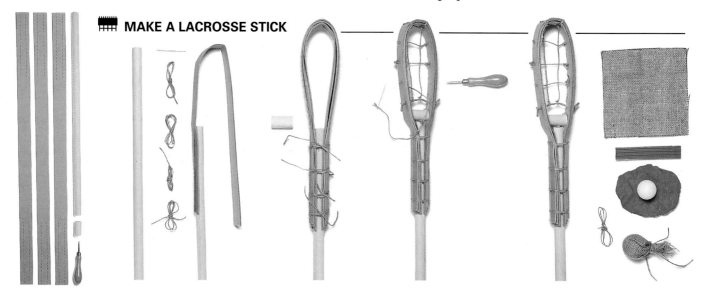

You will need: broomstick or thick dowel, strong cardboard, ping-pong ball, string, glue, awl, saw, square of burlap, modeling clay

1 Ask an adult to help you cut three strips of cardboard and to cut the handle and spacer bar from the dowel. Bend one strip of cardboard around and carefully glue both ends to the handle, as shown.

2 Repeat this with the other two strips, until you have a loop made of three thicknesses of cardboard. (The Native Americans would have used strips of hide.) Use string to tie the loop securely in place.

3 Push in the spacer bar at the top of the handle and glue it into place. Use the awl very carefully to make holes around the loop.

4 Thread string through the holes to make the net, as shown. Knot the ends on the outside of the loop to hold the net in place.

5 To make the ball, flatten the clay and wrap it tightly around the ping-pong ball. Cover it with the square of fabric and tie tightly with string. (Native Americans used a ball of animal hair covered with hide.)

GAMBLING GAMES were very popular with women, who sometimes played for very high stakes, such as offering to become a slave to the other player. Games were more often played for furs, skins, household goods, moccasins, or horses.

POST BALL was played just for fun by both men and women. They set up a post in the village square and the object was to hit the post with a ball. The women could use their hands, but the men could use only sticks.

▽ picking up the ball

◁ throwing the ball

△ tackling, or checking, to get the ball from another player's net

WAR'S LITTLE BROTHER was a fearsome game. It is still played today, in a much more controlled form known as lacrosse. In the past, up to 100 people could play on each team. The playing field had no boundaries and the goals could be over 100 yards wide. Players had to hurl a ball through the goalposts, and the game was won by the first team to score 12 goals. It often lasted for hours. There were no rules of fair play, so it was often a bloody battle with many casualties. Players were pushed, beaten with sticks, often badly injured, and sometimes killed.

△ players jumping to catch the ball in their nets

THE AWL GAME was a game of chance. The board was marked out on a blanket. Each player pinned an awl (a tool used for piercing hides) through the blanket in various places. They moved their awls around the blanket in opposite directions.

FOUR STICKS were thrown at the central stone to decide each move. One carried a special mark. If a stick fell flat side up, it counted for one move. If the mark came up, it meant an extra throw. The board showed dry and flowing rivers. Dry rivers were safe, but players who fell in flowing rivers or on an opponent's position had to go back to the start.

MUSIC AND DANCE were central to the Native American way of life and everybody took part. People believed that music was the language of the spirits. Mothers sang lullabies to their children, warriors sang to call upon their guardian spirits, hunters made magic animal music, and farmers chanted to their crops. There were ceremonial songs for births, marriages, deaths, and funerals.

▷ *These Ute musicians and dancers in the Great Basin and Plateau area were photographed in 1900.*

RATTLES, RASPS, AND DRUMS were used to create rhythms. Turtle shells, coconuts, gourds, and buffalo horns were natural percussion instruments. People made other instruments from wood or hide. A gourd rattle's sound could be improved by putting pebbles or beans inside, along with a few of the original seeds to help the rattle keep its spiritual powers.

rattle

🛖 MAKE A RATTLE

You will need: dried beans or peas, a tennis ball, a dowel (10 in. long), glue, paper, paint, thick string, colored raffia

1 Make holes on either side of the tennis ball, put the beans inside, and push the dowel through, as shown.

2 Tear the paper into pieces and glue them onto the ball in a smooth papier-mâché layer. When the glue has dried, wind the string around the handle and ball, gluing it in place as you go. Leave a gap around the middle of the ball.

3 Decorate the rattle by painting a pattern on the plain part of the ball and adding a raffia tail.

⛟ MAKE A DRUM AND DRUMSTICK

You will need: a flower pot, glue, canvas, thin string, paints, felt-tip pens, two thin sticks or dowels, modeling clay, string, raffia

1 Cut a curved piece of fabric to fit around the pot and glue it on. Cut another piece to fit over the top and to reach well down the sides.

2 Braid or twist the string to make a decorative cord. Stretch the fabric over the pot and use the cord to tie it firmly in place just below the rim.

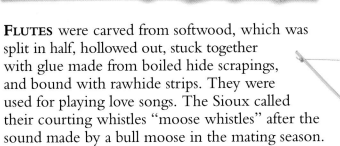

flute

FLUTES were carved from softwood, which was split in half, hollowed out, stuck together with glue made from boiled hide scrapings, and bound with rawhide strips. They were used for playing love songs. The Sioux called their courting whistles "moose whistles" after the sound made by a bull moose in the mating season.

WHISTLES made music for war. Warriors rode into battle blowing whistles made from eagle bones. Eagles symbolized courage.

SONGS were not complicated. They often had a simple tune, usually going down the scale from high notes to low notes. Songs and chants were owned by the person who made them up. If the singer had enjoyed a long and happy life, the right to sing the song would be passed on to the family or even sold for a high price.

△ *A group in California called the Maidu made a simple musical bow. The player plucked the single string, changing the pitch of the note by opening and closing his or her mouth.*

THROBBING DRUMS were like a heartbeat to these peoples. Their sounds were sacred, particularly that of the water drum, which could only be played by those thought worthy, such as distinguished warriors.

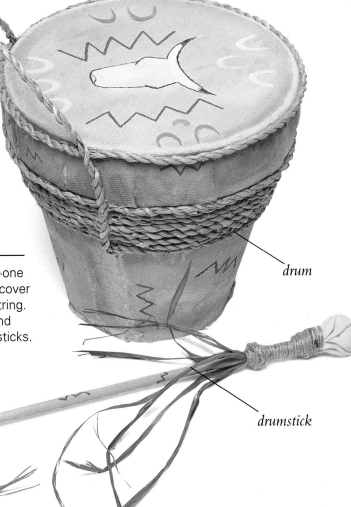

drum

4 Stick balls of clay to one end of each stick and cover with fabric tied with string. Decorate with raffia and paint patterns on the sticks.

3 Finish off with a loop of cord for a handle. Paint the drum to make the cloth look like buffalo hide. Wetting the fabric with paint will shrink it and improve the tone of the drum. Use felt-tip pens to decorate the drum.

drumstick

Artwork

In some cultures, art represents real things. For Native Americans, art was more than that. It was a way of expressing their hopes and fears, of thanking the creator for gifts, and of pleasing the creator with prayers and promises. Because of this, their art was symbolic. It used symbols and signs to represent their ideas, beliefs, dreams, and visions. When artists drew an animal or a person, they were trying to show the inner spirit, not the outer appearance.

△ *This California Karok basket maker was photographed in 1896. She is using the twining method, rather than the coiling technique shown below.*

BASKETS were made by almost all Native Americans, but those of the Southwest and California were particularly skillful weavers. They used baskets for everything from cradles, storage chests, and sieves to bird and fish traps, backpacks, hats, and mats. Some were so tightly woven that they were waterproof and could even be used for brewing beer. Materials used included rushes, bear grass, yucca leaves, and willow, which were steamed until the fibers were supple. Symbolic designs were woven into the baskets using fibers that were colored with mineral or vegetable dyes.

MAKE A BASKET

You will need: thick twine or plaited string, raffia, darning needle

1 Thread the needle with a length of raffia. You will need several lengths to make the basket.

2 Begin the basket base by coiling the twine or plaited string tightly. Work outward from the center. Sew each layer to the last one as you build up the coils.

3 Once you have a flat base, about five coils wide, begin to build up the sides of the basket. Finish off by sewing down the end of the twine securely.

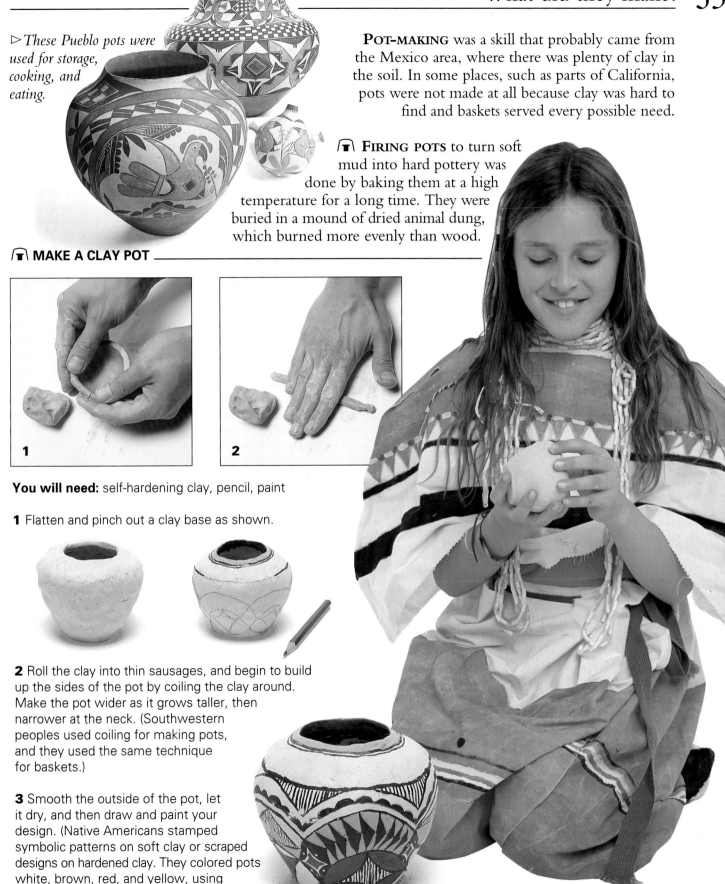

▷ *These Pueblo pots were used for storage, cooking, and eating.*

POT-MAKING was a skill that probably came from the Mexico area, where there was plenty of clay in the soil. In some places, such as parts of California, pots were not made at all because clay was hard to find and baskets served every possible need.

⬀ **FIRING POTS** to turn soft mud into hard pottery was done by baking them at a high temperature for a long time. They were buried in a mound of dried animal dung, which burned more evenly than wood.

⬀ **MAKE A CLAY POT**

1

2

You will need: self-hardening clay, pencil, paint

1 Flatten and pinch out a clay base as shown.

2 Roll the clay into thin sausages, and begin to build up the sides of the pot by coiling the clay around. Make the pot wider as it grows taller, then narrower at the neck. (Southwestern peoples used coiling for making pots, and they used the same technique for baskets.)

3 Smooth the outside of the pot, let it dry, and then draw and paint your design. (Native Americans stamped symbolic patterns on soft clay or scraped designs on hardened clay. They colored pots white, brown, red, and yellow, using pigments from the earth.)

TEXTILES have been woven in North America for two thousand years. Very early cloth was not woven on a loom. The threads were made by spinning fibers from plants and animal hair. Then they were woven together by knitting, crocheting, plaiting, and twining in many different ways.

THE DYES AND PAINTS used by Native Americans were made from minerals and plants. Minerals are found in different colored soils. Iron in soil gives a range of reds, yellows, and browns. Soil with copper makes greens and blues. Graphite makes black; and clay, limestone, and gypsum make white. Color can also be taken from plants, berries, roots, moss, and bark. Boiling or soaking the materials with the plant changes their color.

DESIGNS AND COLORS had different meanings for different groups, and even for individual artists. Sometimes the artist had a dream that showed him or her what designs and colors to use. Although it is difficult to say exactly what particular colors meant, there were some general uses:

Blue	Female, moon, sky, water, thunder, sadness
Black	Male, cold, night, disease, death, underworld
Green	Earth, summer, rain, plants
Red	War, day, blood, wounds, sunset
White	Winter, death, snow
Yellow	Day, dawn, sunshine

DYEING FABRIC

turmeric makes bright yellow

onion skin makes yellowish brown

blueberries make mauve

avocado skin makes pink

You will need: white cotton fabric, piece of muslin, string, ingredients for color (see left), cutting board, knife, old pan, wooden spoon, pitcher or bowl, strainer

1 Choose the colors you want to dye your fabric and prepare the ingredients. Place them on the muslin and tie into a bundle with the string.

2 Put the fabric and muslin bundle into the pan. Cover with water and ask an adult to help you boil it.

3 When the fabric has changed color, let the dye cool and strain it into the pitcher so you can reuse it.

4 Let the fabric dry naturally. Remember that the color will fade and run if you wash it.

▷ *Chilkat dance blankets were worn by Tlingit people for ceremonies (see page 38). They were decorated with stylized symbols representing animals.*

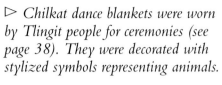

tail and wing shape of a bird

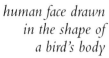
human face drawn in the shape of a bird's body

frog's head

bear's legs and paws

bird's feet

head of a brown bear

FRINGES appeared in the decoration of almost all their clothes and artwork. A fringe was the symbol for rain, which was said to be a blessing because it made plants grow, but also a curse because it could make life so damp and uncomfortable.

SHAPES AND SYMBOLS that people used for decoration varied from one area to another:

  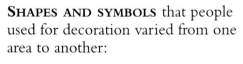 

Southeast   *Southwest*   *Northeast*   *Northwest*   *California*   *Plains*

CURVES AND SPIRALS were popular in the Southeast, where bird and animal shapes were often used.

PARALLEL LINES as well as curves featured in the cultures of the Southwest.

THE FLOWING LINES of plant and flower shapes were used by people in the Northeast.

BIRDS, FISH, AND HUMAN FACES featured in the Northwest, often within a curved shape.

TRIANGLES, RECTANGLES, AND SQUARES were used in many designs in California, especially for basketwork.

GEOMETRIC SHAPES, particularly triangles, were popular on the Plains.

SIMPLE LOOMS with a fixed warp (the vertical threads) were used in ancient times in the Southwest. Later, people in this area developed the true loom. It had a pair of horizontal sticks separating every other thread of the warp. The weft (the horizontal threads) could then be pushed through from side to side with a shuttle, making weaving much easier and quicker.

THE CHILKAT, a branch of the Tlingit nation, were expert weavers. In their homelands, there were no flocks of fleecy sheep and no wild cotton, just mountains and cedar trees. People wove with the hair of wild mountain goats and shredded fibers from the soft inner bark of cedar trees. A blanket took up to a year to make.

MAKE A SIMPLE WEAVING FRAME

You will need: strips of wood (8 in. and 14 in.), glue, pencil, ruler, small nails, hammer, large yarn needle or bodkin, colored yarn

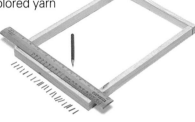

1 Glue and nail the strips of wood to make the frame, as shown. Measure and mark positions for the nails at each end. Make them evenly spaced, about $1/5$ in. apart. Ask an adult to help you hammer the nails in.

2 To make the warp, tie a piece of yarn to the first nail at one corner. Stretch it back and forth across the frame, looping it around the nails. Tie it off on the last nail.

3 To make the weft, thread a length of colored yarn through the needle and wind it around as shown.

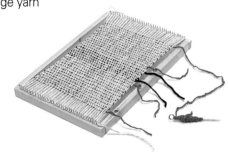

4 Tie the loose end of the yarn to the outside warp thread, then weave the needle in and out from side to side.

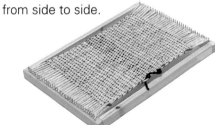

5 When you want to change color, tie the new yarn to the outside warp thread as before.

6 When you have filled the frame, tie the end of your last weft row to the outside warp thread and carefully lift your finished piece off the nails. Tie together the two loops at each corner.

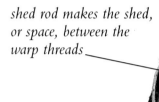

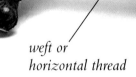

shed rod makes the shed, or space, between the warp threads

heddle rod holds the warp threads in place and changes them back and forth

shuttle

breast beam

weft or horizontal thread

⊺\ THE SPIDERWOMAN was a spirit who wove webs to catch rain clouds and had taught the first people on Earth how to weave. Weavers in the Southwest used the symbol of the spiderwoman in their designs as a way of thanking her for the knowledge that she had passed on to them.

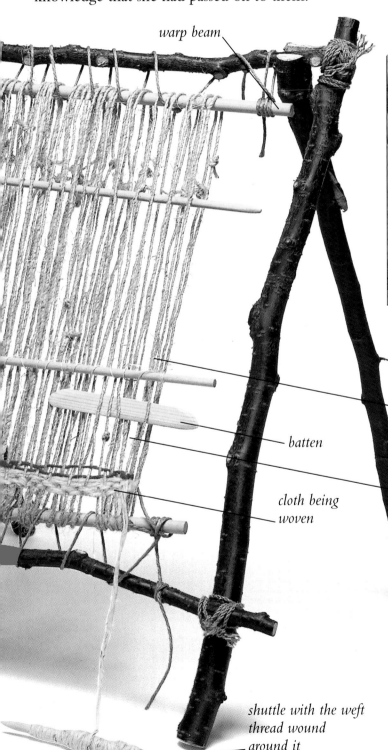

warp beam

warp or vertical thread

batten

weaving frame

cloth being woven

shed, or space where the shuttle passes through

shuttle with the weft thread wound around it

△ *The present-day Navajo weave using the traditional methods and designs.*

⊺\ THE NAVAJO are perhaps best known for their beautifully woven blankets with strong, geometric designs. The ideas for the designs, it is said, came directly from the weaver's inner spirit. The women who made them boasted that their blankets were so closely woven, they could hold water. They always made a tiny mistake in the weaving, as they believed if they were ever to make one perfect thing, their lives would be complete and their time on Earth would be over.

Transportation

Walking was the main way of getting around on land until the Europeans brought horses to North America. Native Americans had developed backpacks and baskets to help them carry things more easily. When they traveled by water, they found that every lake, river, or sea presented different problems, so each kind of water had its own type of boat.

🏠 **SEAWORTHY BOATS** were built by Native Americans living along the Northwest Coast. Large, strong, straight cedar trees grew there, and they were cut down, dug out, and shaped to suit deep ocean waters and the shallows off the coast. Large dugouts, with high, curved ends to keep inshore waves from splashing aboard, were used for trading runs up and down the coast. For fishing and whaling trips in the open sea, people built bigger, stronger boats with straighter sides.

🛶 **BUFFALO-HIDE CANOES** were round river craft made of hide stretched over a wooden frame. They were made by people on the edge of the Plains, where there were few trees for building boats.

TRADING was the main reason for traveling. Apart from the Plains nations, which followed herds of buffalo, people usually stayed close to the territory in which they were born. Some did move between summer and winter villages, some traveled to wage war on neighboring groups, and some journeyed to attend gatherings and ceremonies.

platform from which hunters could spear fish

high bow to keep waves out

carved or painted decoration, often representing animals, to show the owner's importance

🏠 **CANOE-MAKING TOOLS** included stone and bone axes, adzes, gouges, and wedges that were used to hollow out cedar logs. To soften the wood for final shaping, the logs were sometimes filled with water, and hot stones or a carefully controlled fire would be used to burn away the inside.

△ *Seagoing canoes were dug out from a single tree. Some could carry up to 60 men.*

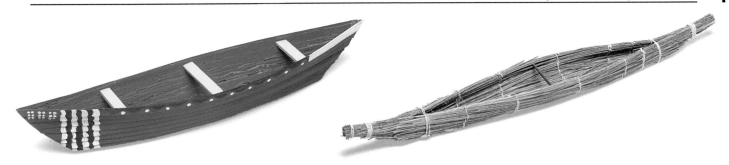

PLANK BOATS were built for sea journeys by the Chumash of Southern California. They used hand-split planks, making little holes in them so they could lash them together with leather thongs or plant fibers. They waterproofed them with tar.

REED RAFTS were light, easy-to-carry, canoe-shaped boats used by Californian groups. They were made from reeds tied together in bundles.

wooden seat or thwart

wooden paddle

interior painted with tar to make it waterproof

THE PRICE OF GOODS traded by Native Americans went up and down according to supply and demand. When something is plentiful, it is worth less, and when there is little available, the price goes up. These values applied when there were few horses and many buffalo:

8 buffalo robes   = 1 ordinary horse
5 buffalo robes   = 1 bear-claw necklace
1 buffalo robe   = 36 iron arrowheads

GOODS FOR TRADING varied from nation to nation, but included some of the following items:

- Baskets, acorns, seaweed, dried fish, shells
- Dried fish and fish oil, salt, boats and dugouts, copper and silver jewelry
- Hides, horses, eagle feathers
- Blankets, wool, dyes, jewelry
- Shells, wampum, furs, copper and copper tools, pearls
- Tobacco, shells, pearls

BOATS OF DIFFERENT SHAPES were built for different conditions. Native Americans living by lakes and rivers needed easy-to-steer, lightweight canoes that could be taken out of the water and carried when it became too dangerous or shallow. Small canoes were perfect for shooting over waterfalls, but larger boats were needed for carrying goods for trading. A boat with a low bow and stern is good in calm waters. A high bow and stern give protection from rough waters but slow the boat down because of greater wind resistance.

gunwale   *decorative stitching*

wooden paddle

🏠 **BIRCH TREES** were plentiful in the Northeast and the Great Lakes area. These tall, thin, straight trees are wrapped in up to nine layers of bark that comes off in sheets when carefully peeled. The outer skin is thick and white, the inner skins thinner, browner, and softer.

🏠 **CANOE BARK** was peeled from a cut tree in the spring, when the outer layer is at its thickest. It was used, brown side out and white side in, to cover a frame of cedarwood. The bark sheets were sewn together with spruce roots. The seams were then made waterproof with a covering of gummy sap from the pine tree, heated until it became a thick, gooey syrup.

🏠 **PADDLES** were shaped from wood, anchors made from stones, bails from shells, and ropes from plant fiber or strips of hide. Native Americans saw no need for sails on their boats. They did not particularly want to go where the wind blew them, so paddles were all they needed for their short fishing and trading trips.

🏠 **MAKE A BIRCH BARK CANOE**

You will need: thick and thin balsa wood strips, bulldog clips, craft knife, pencil, needle, thread, paints, glue

1 Take the thick strip of balsa (about 16 in. long), mark out the gunwale (the top part) of the canoe as shown, and cut it out carefully, using a craft knife.

2 Soak the thin strips of balsa in hot water for half an hour. Lay the gunwale over the strips and fold them upward to make the sides of the canoe. Lift the gunwale into position and glue it to the top of the sides, using clips to hold it in place.

3 When dry, cut off any balsa sticking out above the gunwale. Glue on a thin finishing strip and sew it in place as shown.

4 Sew thin strips of balsa wood together to make ends of the canoe.

 BIRCH BARK CANOES were light, portable boats made of bark stretched over a frame of saplings. They were used by the Algonquian peoples who lived, hunted, and fished on the wooded shores and winding waterways around the Great Lakes. The design of their canoe remains practically unchanged. It came in two versions, a low-ended one for the rivers and a high-ended one for rougher waters.

△ *This member of the Chippewa nation is building a birch bark canoe in the forests of the Northeast.*

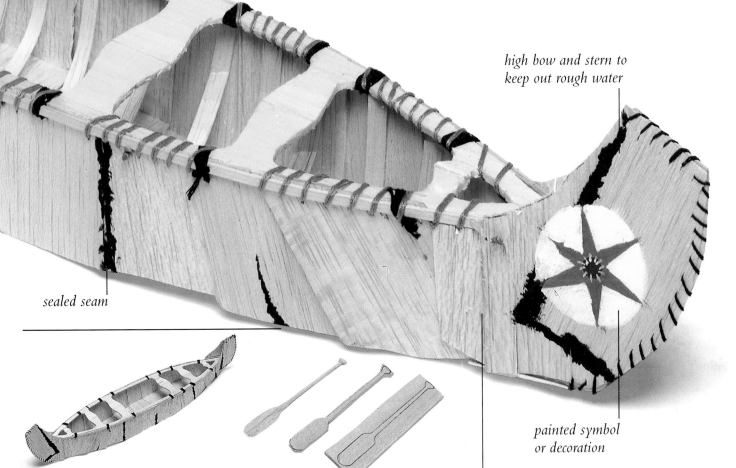

high bow and stern to keep out rough water

sealed seam

painted symbol or decoration

5 Glue the ends in place, then paint all the seams black (like the sap the Algonquians used for waterproofing).

6 Put thin reinforcing strips inside the canoe as shown. Decorate the canoe with stitching and motifs.

7 Cut a round-bladed paddle from the thick sheet of balsa wood, as shown. These paddles were designed for shooting rapids, because a rounded end is less likely to be damaged by stones and rocks.

overlapping bark pieces pointed toward the stern to help the water flow easily around the canoe

BEFORE THE HORSE was brought to North America about 400 years ago, all land journeys were made on foot. Anything that needed to be carried was hauled by women, or by dogs pulling a **travois** made from two tepee poles attached to a harness. Native Americans following a buffalo herd on foot covered only about six miles a day. They had few possessions, and they kept their tepees small so they were easy to carry.

enemy killed in hand combat   hail   warrior wore breastplate   coup marks

△ *Plains warriors decorated their horses with painted symbols.*

MAKE A TRAVOIS

You will need: twigs, string, plain fabric, paints, paintbrush, glue, model horse

1 Use two long twigs and two short crosspieces to make the basic shape, as shown. Tie them securely.

2 Cut thin strips of fabric and weave them to make a carrying platform. Glue to the frame. (Plains people tied a travois with strips of buffalo hide.)

3 Wind string around the length of the poles and glue it. (On the Plains, strips of hide were used for this, to stop the horse's skin from chafing.)

AFTER THE HORSE was brought to the Americas by Spanish settlers, life for Plains nations was transformed. They used horses to move swiftly in battle, to outrun buffalo, and to pull the travois. A camp could now move 30 miles in one day. Tepees became bigger and more spacious. Women no longer had to carry heavy loads, and they had more time for leisure and for making things. People owned more and could transport things more easily.

4 Bend and glue thin twigs to form a cage on the platform. Cut and paint a piece of fabric for the horse blanket. Paint symbols on the horse. Tie the poles and blanket to its back.

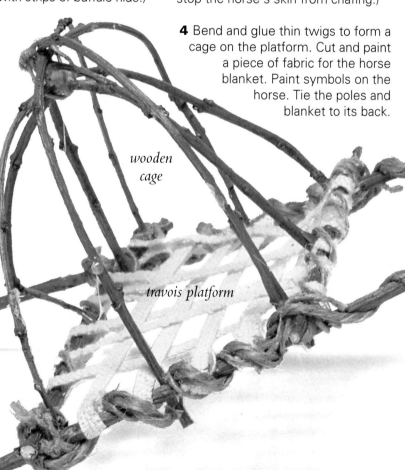

wooden cage

travois platform

A SIOUX SONG tells of the respect and honor with which Plains warriors treated their horses:
'My horse be swift in flight
Even like a bird:
My horse be swift in flight.
Bear me now in safety
Far from the enemy's arrows
And you shall be rewarded
With streamers and ribbons red.'

△ *Young children often rode on a travois. Sometimes a wooden cage was put over the platform to keep passengers and possessions from falling off.*

▲ BABIES were carried on cradle boards by their mothers. They were tightly wrapped up and strapped to the boards with leather thongs, so that they could not wriggle around and could be kept warm and safe.

▲ SADDLES AND BRIDLES were made from buffalo hide and hair. A braided buffalo-hair rope or a thin strip of rawhide looped around the horse's lower jaw was all Plains riders needed to control their horses. While out hunting or fighting they rode bareback or used a simple hide saddle stuffed with buffalo hair. Women had wooden saddles padded with hide. Stirrups were made from wood, steamed into shape, and covered in rawhide. Wealthy horse owners often had their **tack** decorated with paint and beads.

▲ TRAVOIS were made by women. The women took pride in their craftswork; they were thought to be bad wives if their hide straps were cut unevenly or, worse still, had hair on them.

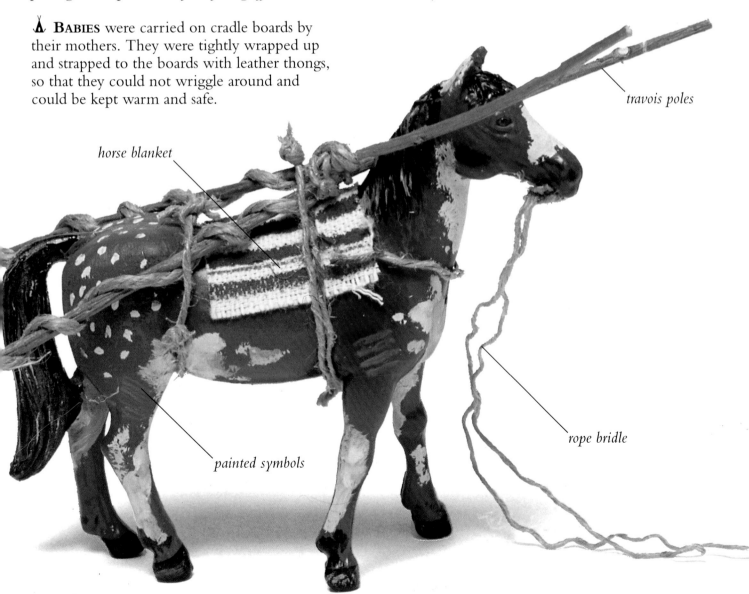

horse blanket

travois poles

rope bridle

painted symbols

Hunting and Warfare

Native American hunters needed to be brave, confident, and skillful. If they were successful, they were rewarded with glory and praise. For Native Americans, the respect given to successful hunters was perhaps the most important thing in life. Before the European invasion, arguments over hunting grounds and raids for horses were some of the reasons for setting out on the warpath. Some nations viewed warfare as a chance to appear heroic. However, many sought peace rather than war.

△ *This Plains warrior was an Arapaho chief in 1870.*

war club

NATIVE AMERICAN warriors crept up on the enemy quickly and quietly, attacked fiercely, then turned and ran for it. There was no shame in retreat.

coup stick

⚔ BRAVERY was measured by how close warriors got to their enemy. Riding in close to touch the enemy with a coup was called counting coup. It was seen as more courageous than killing at 50 yards with a bow and arrow.

⚔ A BOW WITH ARROWS was the most widely used weapon. The Sioux made bows from ash wood, with a bow string made of two twisted sinews. A war bow could be fired more quickly than a gun and be deadly accurate from over 100 yards away.

⚔ MAKE A BOW AND ARROW

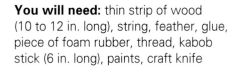

You will need: thin strip of wood (10 to 12 in. long), string, feather, glue, piece of foam rubber, thread, kabob stick (6 in. long), paints, craft knife

1 Mark the bow as shown, and shape and nick the ends as shown. Use the craft knife carefully.

2 Make a loop in the string, thread it into the nick at one end, and tie it to the other end, bending the bow a little as shown.

3 Wrap and glue two lengths of string around the bow to make a handgrip as shown.

4 Make flights for the arrow by splitting the spine of the feather and cutting out three small sections as shown above.

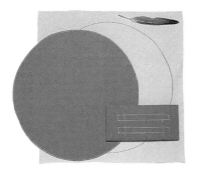
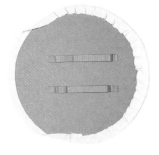
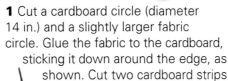

You will need: strong cardboard, plain fabric, feathers, raffia, paint, pencil, awl, glue

1 Cut a cardboard circle (diameter 14 in.) and a slightly larger fabric circle. Glue the fabric to the cardboard, sticking it down around the edge, as shown. Cut two cardboard strips as handles and glue to the back of the shield.

2 Draw a design on the front of the shield and paint it. Make small holes in the shield with the awl, thread raffia through them, and tie on feathers as decoration.

⚑ **RAWHIDE SHIELDS** were painted with signs and kept wrapped up before battle so the power would not leak away.

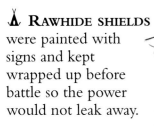

war ax

spear

▦ **TOMAHAWKS** were curved, light, axes used in hand-to-hand combat. They could also be thrown with fearsome force and accuracy.

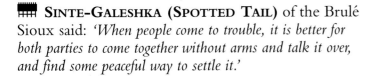

▦ **SINTE-GALESHKA (SPOTTED TAIL)** of the Brulé Sioux said: *'When people come to trouble, it is better for both parties to come together without arms and talk it over, and find some peaceful way to settle it.'*

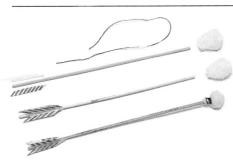

5 Glue the flights onto the kabob stick as shown. Cut the arrow to half the length of the bow. Stick a small ball of foam rubber onto the cut end of the arrow and secure it with thread.

6 Paint and decorate both the bow and the arrow. Plains warriors painted pictures of their enemies on their arrows, so the arrows would know where to go. You can dip the arrow tips into water-soluble paint and fire them at a target.

NEVER FIRE AN ARROW AT ANYONE. EVEN A TOY ARROW CAN CAUSE AN INJURY.

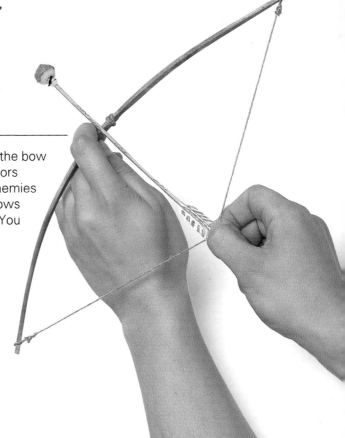

Communication

As recently as 200 years ago, there were over 300 languages spoken in North America. None of these had any links to languages that were spoken in Europe, Asia, or Africa. Families belonging to the same nation did not necessarily speak the same language, and people who shared a language were often spread over a wide area, because of trade and mobile ways of life. So Native Americans developed sign language to help them communicate with their neighbors. It allowed them to express emotions, as well as warnings and signals.

SIGN LANGUAGE used by Native Americans was made up of a mixture of mime and signaling, based on actions and shapes of things rather than on sounds. When Plains people visited Europe in the last century, they found they could communicate easily and naturally with deaf people.

EARLY EUROPEAN EXPLORERS and settlers tried to write down the sounds of Native American words, but some just could not be conveyed using our alphabet. Some Native American words became familiar place names:

Place	Pronunciation	Meaning
Alabama	alba–amo	plant reapers
Dakota	dak–hota	the friendly ones
Canada	kanata	cabin
Illinois	ili–ni–wak	men
Idaho	ee–dah–how	behold! the sun coming down the mountain
Iowa	aayahooweewa	sleepy
Kentucky	ken–tah–teh	land of tomorrow
Minnesota	minne–sota	cloudy water
Texas	tiesha	friend

 **PLAINS SIGN LANGUAGE**

Native American—stroke hand twice

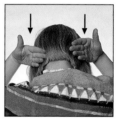
Cheyenne—chop at left index finger

Comanche—imitate motion of snake

Crow—hold fist to forehead, palm down

Osage—move hands down back of head

Pawnee—make V sign and extend hand

Nez Perce—move finger under nose

Sioux—drag hand across neck

alone—move right hand to the right

buffalo

cannot—move finger along palm and down

horse

bad—make fist, then open downward

moon

opposite

Caught the Enemy   *Eagle Horse*   *He Dog*   *Kills by the Camp*   *Spotted Face*   *Stabber*

△ *Native American names were meaningful. People were often named after an animal or a special event in their lives (see page 54). These* **pictographs** *of names were used as signatures by the Sioux.*

SMOKE SIGNALS were sent by hunters and warriors in the flat, open Plains country, on clear days when no wind blew. By flapping a blanket across the column of smoke from a fire, they made combinations of long and short puffs to tell of the presence of buffalo or the approach of enemies. The system was far from reliable.

▷ *A Sioux girl and a Nez Perce boy would have been able to speak to one another using sign language.*

In the early nineteenth century, Sequoya developed a writing system for the Cherokee language. His alphabet contained 85 characters, and each one represented a syllable, or unit, from which a word is made ("syl-la-ble" has three units).

LANGUAGE WAS SPOKEN, not written. For centuries, Native Americans passed down many stories and traditions by word of mouth. Since they did not put their thoughts on paper, they developed fantastic memories and were good at telling stories and making speeches. They used their spoken languages in beautiful, moving ways.

THE MAIN REASON that we know today about the rich spoken tradition of the Native Americans is because of the powerful speeches that were made by their chiefs and leaders in **post-contact** times. Many speeches were about their sadness at losing their lands and at the white people's wasteful ways with nature.

CHIEF SEATTLE made a speech when the city of Seattle was founded on the lands of the Duwamish in 1855. He said: *'There was a time when our people covered the whole land as the waves of the wind-ruffled sea cover its shell-paved floor... Every hillside, every valley, every plain and grove has been hallowed by some sad or happy event in days long vanished. Even the rocks, which seem to be dumb and dead as they swelter in the sun along the silent shore, thrill with memories of events connected with the lives of my people, and the very dust upon which you now stand... is rich with the blood of our ancestors.'*

SEQUOYA'S CHEROKEE ALPHABET was the only written form of Native American language. Sequoyah (1760-1843) dreamed of giving his people the power of the written word that the Europeans used so well. It was a great success. Every Cherokee man, woman, and child saw how useful reading and writing could be. They began producing their own newspapers, both in Cherokee and in English.

Pictographs were often painted on hide or carved into wood and then colored. Some Northeastern people used this technique to make calendar sticks.

PICTOGRAPHS AND IDEOGRAMS were used in **precontact** times to leave messages and records of historical facts. Pictographs were simple drawings used to represent people, animals, objects, or events that had taken place. Ideograms were symbols that stood for abstract ideas, such as love, longing, hatred, or sadness.

WINTER COUNTS recorded the passing years by focusing on particularly important events that everybody in the group remembered. These might include an outbreak of illness or the sighting of a spectacular comet. Plains peoples painted their winter counts on buffalo hides.

MAKE YOUR OWN WINTER COUNT

You will need: paints, paintbrush, pencil, plain fabric (about 24 x 24 in.)

1 Cut the fabric to the shape of a buffalo hide, as shown. Paint it off-white, to look like hide.

2 Make up your own symbols to remind you of important events. Choose one for each week to sum up the main event of that week, such as playing a sport, getting measles, or having a birthday.

3 Paint your symbols on the canvas, starting at the center of a spiral as shown.

Pictographs used by the Dakota Sioux:

smallpox epidemic

shower of meteors

village attacked and inhabitants killed

peace with a rival nation

successful horse raid

new settlement

Religion

The unseen spirit world was very real to Native Americans. They believed that the natural world and the spirit world were joined together on Earth. Everything in their lives—the rising of the sun in the morning, people's success at hunting, and the health of their children—was controlled by major and minor gods and spirits. They recognized the power of these spirits in everything they did and said.

▦ **THREE WORLDS** made up the universe, according to Southeastern nations. They believed that an Upper World, a Lower World, and This World were separate but linked. This World, in which humans, plants, and most animals lived, was a round island resting on water. It hung from the sky on four cords attached at the north, south, west, and east. The Upper World was pure, perfect, and predictable; the Lower World was full of chaos and change. This World was balanced between the two. Spirits moved freely between the Worlds, and people had the privilege of helping the spirits keep the Worlds in balance.

⛪ MAKE A SPIRIT MASK

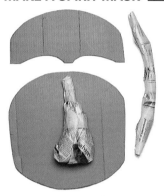
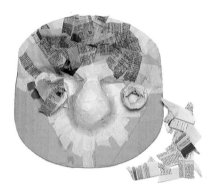

You will need: cardboard, masking tape, newspapers, papier-mâché, paint, raffia, elastic, glue, hook-and-loop fasteners

1 Cut basic shapes for the mask and forehead from cardboard. Tape on a paper nose and eyebrows.

2 Tape the forehead to the mask, using crumpled paper to fill it and build the forehead out. Make eye sockets from rings of folded paper. Cut cardboard ears and tape into place.

3 Paste strips of paper over the shapes. Allow to dry.

4 Paint the mask white, then add your design in color. Glue on raffia for the hair.

5 Use cardboard, crumpled paper, and papier-mâché to build different mouth shapes. Attach them to the basic mask with fasteners.

The Kwakiutl made masks of the spirit Echo with a different mouth for each creature they believed he could imitate.

basic mask

the spirit of Echo himself

an eagle or a raven

a bear

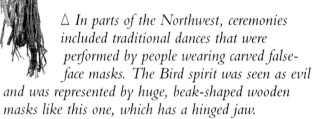

△ *In parts of the Northwest, ceremonies included traditional dances that were performed by people wearing carved false-face masks. The Bird spirit was seen as evil and was represented by huge, beak-shaped wooden masks like this one, which has a hinged jaw.*

STORIES OF HOW THE WORLD BEGAN were told by most Native Americans. Pueblos believed creation was the work of the Spider Grandmother. Some Northwestern nations believed it was the Raven, while others believed that the world was made by a number of assorted spirits. Their neighbors in the Plateau region saw the world as a clever joke played by their Coyote god. Southeastern people gave the credit to the Master of Breath who lived on high.

VISION QUESTS were an attempt to get personal power from the spirits, instead of relying on the medicine men and women, or **shaman**. Young people went off alone, fasting, sometimes hurting themselves on purpose, and keeping awake until they saw visions. The visions gave them a key to getting the spirits' help for the rest of their lives.

△ **BLACK ELK** said this about his visions: *'I saw more than I can tell, and I understood more than I saw; for I was seeing in a sacred manner the shapes of all things in the spirit.'*

FALSE-FACE MASKS were made by medicine men and women for the Iroquois. They believed that illness was caused by unkind spirits with horrible faces and no bodies who lived in the forest spreading sickness. The cure was to confuse the spirits, so they cut mask shapes from living trees and gave them gruesome faces. Then the shaman danced while wearing the masks until the bewildered spirits left the area.

RITES OF PASSAGE are **rituals** that mark the important stages in a person's life. For example, many people mark the birth of a child with a naming ceremony, a marriage with a wedding ceremony, and a death with a funeral. For most early civilizations, the most important ceremony of all was the celebration of puberty, which is the time when a child becomes an adult. For Native Americans, this meant that young people no longer needed to be protected and could contribute fully to their group.

⚇ **A BABY WAS NAMED** a few days after it was born. A respected warrior would be paid, usually in horses, to name the baby. The child's given name often reflected some glorious action in the warrior's past, but it would be changed when the child made a mark for itself and earned its own name.

△ *The Southwestern Hopi wore* **kachina** *masks when they performed certain festive dances.*

🔺 MAKE A KACHINA DOLL

You will need: polystyrene foam (12 x 3 x 1 in.), acrylic paints, yarn, fine sandpaper, craft knife, raffia

1 Draw an outline on the foam.

2 Carve out the shape carefully with a craft knife, as shown. When the basic shape is cut, use sandpaper to smooth and round off the edges.

3 Paint a face and clothes on your doll, and add your own designs. Decorate waist and wrists with raffia and colored yarn.

🔺 **BECOMING AN ADULT** was tough. Boys as young as 10 would have to prove that they were made of strong stuff. Yuma boys had to run 10 to 15 miles a day for four days, with no sleep or food. Girls had to lie still, face down, on a bed of warm sand for four days while friends and relatives made long speeches.

🔺 **MARRIAGE** was mostly a free choice. In the Pueblo nation, the bridegroom moved in with his wife's family, but he could be sent home to his own family if things did not work out. Husbands and wives were expected to be faithful while their marriages lasted. A bridegroom was expected to weave his bride's wedding clothes.

Tawa, who was associated with the sun

THE KACHINAS brought help from the spirits, who were everywhere and in everything, controlling every part of Pueblo life. The spirit world and the real world could not be separated. People wore kachina masks in their ceremonies, to represent the spirits. Children were given kachina dolls to help them understand the spirit world and identify kachinas.

Sio Calako, a giant spirit

Eototo, chief of the kachinas

AT THE END of their lives, Native Americans generally accepted death with little fuss, however it came. As it drew near, people sang their personal death song, which they had rehearsed throughout their lives. The dead were usually cremated or buried in simple, shallow graves or on scaffolds, so they eventually blended back into the earth. Most people believed in a happy afterlife, in a place where the sun shone, crops ripened, and hunting grounds teemed with animals.

SMOKING THE PIPE OF PRAYER was one of the most important rites. People smoked a mixture of tobacco and sweet-smelling herbs in a ceremonial pipe. They believed that the smoke was the very breath of prayer, and the pipe itself was seen as a sacred pathway to the spirit world.

Natural Science

Native Americans respected nature and so did not take from it without giving something back. The many nations hunted and fished carefully so as not to upset nature's balance. They cut down few live trees, and they took only what they needed to survive.

NATIVE AMERICANS UNDERSTOOD NATURE and had a special relationship with it. They watched the seasons come and go. People observed the movements of the stars and planets, the life cycles of plants and trees, and the habits and breeding seasons of the animals they hunted. They believed that these things happened as a result of the work of the spirit world.

⟨▼⟩ MAKE A SAND PAINTING

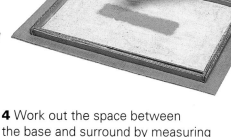

You will need: sand (fine sand is easier to use than builder's sand), water-based powder paints in a variety of colors, bowl, stirring stick, thick cardboard, pencil, craft knife, glue

1 Mix paint and a little water into a thick paste in the bowl. Add a handful of sand and stir.

2 Spoon the mixture onto a piece of cardboard and leave in a warm place until completely dry. Repeat for all colors.

3 Make a sand painting tray. Measure and cut the cardboard (10 x 15 in. base). Make the side pieces by cutting three identical strips of cardboard and gluing them together.

4 Work out the space between the base and surround by measuring the thickness of the sides. Wedge each side into place.

5 Fill your tray with uncolored sand, about a quarter of an inch deep. Taking a pinch of one of your colored sands, trickle it carefully onto the base.

HEALING THE SICK was one of the main tasks of the shaman, or medicine man or woman. Healing was done with herbs and with a lot of ritual, which in itself can often help a sick person to feel better. The Native Americans discovered the healing properties of many plants, including willow bark, which contains salicylic acid, the main ingredient of today's aspirin.

◁ *The Navajo used sand paintings as their main way of treating sick people.*

A CHEROKEE STORY told that people upset the spirits of the animals because they killed them for food and crowded them out of their habitats. The animals took their revenge on humans by creating disease and sickness. But the spirits of the plants, who were people's friends, decided to help out. Each single plant, from the tallest trees down to the tiniest creeping mosses, agreed to produce a remedy that would fight and cure one of the diseases.

6 Gradually build up the different colors in your design. It is important to plan the design and colors before you begin. The design shown here is based on a Navajo sand painting used to cure a sick baby. It would have been painted on the hogan floor spread with a smooth layer of uncolored sand.

SAND PAINTINGS were made by medicine men or women. A sick person sat on the ground while a colored sand picture was created around them. After the ceremony, when the shaman had prayed and chanted, people took a pinch of the colored sand. This young woman is making a sand painting similar to the original sacred ones.

Looking Back

Finding out how people lived in the past needs careful detective work, especially when they left no written records of their lives.

THE FIRST STEP is to gather evidence. To investigate Native American life, we can listen to the stories and memories of their descendants, passed down from generation to generation. We can take account of travelers' tales from the earliest European explorers, who wrote about and drew what they saw. We can also look at the findings of archaeologists, who study the objects that people have left behind, and of anthropologists, who study how people lived their daily lives.

▽ *This model is based on the archaeological dig at the Koster site in western Illinois. The site is named after the farmers on whose land the first finds were made in 1969. Since then, experts have dug through evidence of 15 settlements. The oldest, at about 3 feet below the present level, dates from 9,000 years ago.*

marker post

sorting table

topsoil

levels of soil marked to make a vertical grid

THE SECOND STEP is to use the evidence we have found to draw conclusions about how Native Americans lived many hundreds of years ago. This task may be complicated by the fact that different experts sometimes reach different conclusions. Their pictures of the past do not always match up, and every generation looks at history from a slightly different angle. The past is always much more complicated than we think.

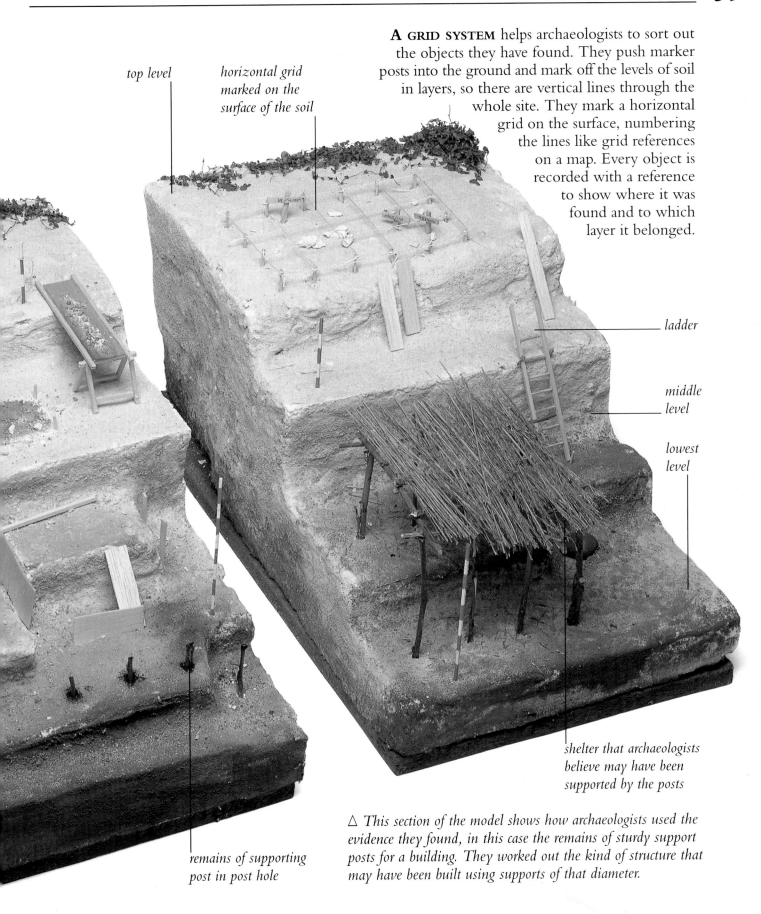

A GRID SYSTEM helps archaeologists to sort out the objects they have found. They push marker posts into the ground and mark off the levels of soil in layers, so there are vertical lines through the whole site. They mark a horizontal grid on the surface, numbering the lines like grid references on a map. Every object is recorded with a reference to show where it was found and to which layer it belonged.

top level

horizontal grid marked on the surface of the soil

ladder

middle level

lowest level

shelter that archaeologists believe may have been supported by the posts

remains of supporting post in post hole

△ This section of the model shows how archaeologists used the evidence they found, in this case the remains of sturdy support posts for a building. They worked out the kind of structure that may have been built using supports of that diameter.

Post-contact Times

Native American history spans about 15,000 years. During this time a number of different cultures have come and gone. But the greatest upheaval that Native Americans have ever faced was the coming of the Europeans, starting with Christopher Columbus in 1492. The Spanish, the Dutch, the French, and the English arrived in waves. They landed in the East and gradually pushed the Native Americans farther and farther west. These new settlers came with guns and they believed the rich, fertile land was theirs for the taking, so they took it.

△ *Chief Red Horse, of the Sioux, drew a series of pictographs representing the Battle of Little Bighorn. This pictograph shows the climax of the battle.*

THE NATIONAL POLICY STATEMENT made by the American government toward Native Americans in 1787 was full of promises that were soon broken. It said:
'The utmost good faith shall always be observed toward the Indians; their lands and property shall never be taken from them without their consent.'

THE NEW SETTLERS, whose ancestors had arrived from Europe, took territorial control from the Native Americans in the East and gradually acquired land in the West. Between 1776 and 1854, the Native Americans were forced back until all their land was lost. By 1912, 48 of the United States had been formed.

◁ *This map shows the stages by which the new settlers took territory over from the Native Americans. Each shaded area shows the land that had been acquired by the date shown.*

△ *Custer hoped to improve his reputation with a victory over the Sioux. His troops, however, were defeated, and the General was killed.*

GEORGE CUSTER was an American General who led his troops into many battles with the Plains peoples over their land and traditional hunting grounds. He grew to respect Native Americans. In 1874, General Custer published a book about his life called *My Life on the Plains*. In it he wrote: *'When the soil which he has claimed and hunted over for so long a time is demanded by this... insatiable monster (modern civilization) there is no appeal; he must yield, or it will roll mercilessly over him, destroying as it advances. Destiny seems to have so willed it, and the world nods its approval.'*

TWO YEARS LATER, in 1876, General Custer and one third of his cavalry regiment were killed in the Battle of Little Bighorn. The soldiers fought against the Sioux nation under its chief, Crazy Horse. This was the Native Americans' greatest victory against the advancing enemies, but in the end it changed nothing.

▷ *The Zuni still produce intricate jewelry from precious stones and silver. This picture was taken in the Southwest in 1970.*

THE LAST OF THE NATIVE AMERICAN WARS was at Wounded Knee in South Dakota in March 1890, when American troops opened fire on a band of Sioux men, women, and children, killing 200 of them. In reality, more Native Americans died of diseases brought by the Europeans, against which they had no defense, than in the wars. In 1890, the last of the Native Americans were driven onto reservations, where land was set aside for their use, but was run by the American government.

TODAY MOST NATIVE AMERICANS live on reservations in the central and western parts of the United States and Canada. At first, reservation life was a nightmare, with traditions and religions banned and children sent away to school to learn European ways. But Native Americans are now much more in control of their own lives. They hand on knowledge of their rich and varied traditions, and reach out to everyone with their unique record of achievements as a nation. Their understanding of the environment and nature's delicate balance is of great importance to people all over the world today.

Glossary

Algonquian nations A group of Northeastern nations who spoke the Algonquian language. There were about 50 different versions of this language.

anthropologist A person who studies the origins, development, and behavior of people.

archaeologist A person who studies remains from the past, such as buildings and possessions.

bolas A rope with weights such as stones attached to it. A bolas was a hunting weapon whirled around to knock birds from the sky or thrown to bring down prey by entangling its legs.

buckskin Animal hide scraped and softened until it looks and feels like the soft, supple skin of a male deer.

canoe A thin, lightweight open boat with pointed ends and no keel. Canoes are pushed through the water by paddles.

chickee A dwelling on stilts with no walls.

civilization A developed and organized group or nation of people.

clan A group of related families.

counting coup (say *coo*) A Native American way of judging a warrior's bravery. The warrior had to come face to face with the enemy and touch him or her with a coup stick. A coup is a sudden act or attack.

culture A group of people living at a particular time in history who believe in the same things and share a way of life.

hogan A hexagonal or octagonal Navajo house made from a log framework plastered with mud.

ideogram A written sign that represents an idea such as love or hate.

igloo A dome-shaped house built from blocks of hard snow or ice.

Iroquois nations A group of Northeastern nations who spoke the Iroquois language. These groups were known in post-contact times as the Five Nations.

kachina Spirits of nature represented by a religious or ceremonial mask or by a doll-like figure.

lacrosse A team sport that originated among Native Americans. It was played using sticks with rawhide nets at the end and a ball made from hair and hide.

livelihood The way a person or group supports itself.

moccasins Shoes or boots made out of animal hide.

pictograph A sign that is written down to represent a person or an object.

post-contact The time in Native American history after the native population had come face to face with explorers and settlers from Europe, Asia, and Africa.

potlatch A Northwestern Native American ceremonial feast, during which many gifts are given to the guests to demonstrate the host's wealth and generosity.

precontact The long period of time before Native Americans had any contact with people from other continents.

pueblo A village of terraced mud houses.

rawhide Stiff animal hide that has been cleaned but is untreated.

ritual A ceremonial way of doing something, such as celebrating an important event.

roach A stiff tuft of animal hair tied on top of the head, worn for decoration.

shaman A man or woman who was believed to have a close relationship with the spirit world. People believed shaman could explain the workings of the gods to them and make their prayers heard.

symbol A visible sign that represents an invisible idea.

tack Equipment, such as bridles and saddles, used for riding horses.

tepee A portable, cone-shaped dwelling of animal skin or bark set over a wooden framework.

terrain The physical characteristics of an area, such as its mountains, rivers, and vegetation.

tomahawk A war club with a rounded end. The word was later used to describe war axes, introduced by Europeans.

totem pole A post that was carved and painted with symbols (usually animals) to represent family members and ancestors.

travois A trailing sled, pulled along by dogs or, later, by horses and used for carrying possessions and people.

wampum Small, white, cylindrical beads made from polished shells and used as money or expensive jewelry.

wickiup A cone-shaped house made from grasses and rushes over a wooden frame.

wigwam A dome- or cone-shaped home made from wooden poles covered with reed or bark mats.

Index